GOSSAMER

A play

by
JOHN MISTO

ORiGiN™
Theatrical

FOR ALL ENQUIRIES CONTACT: ORiGiN™ Theatrical
PO BOX Q1235, QVB Post Office, Sydney, NSW, 1230, Australia
Phone: (61 2) 8514 5201 Fax: (61 2) 9299 2920
enquiries@originmusic.com.au www.origintheatrical.com.au
Part of the ORiGiN™ Music Group
An Australian Independent Music Company

IMPORTANT NOTICE

i

should not be considered to be necessarily endorsing or otherwise attempting to promote an affiliation with any of the owners of the brand names or trademarks or public figures. Such references are solely for use in a dramatic context.

LANGUAGE NOTE

Licensees are welcome to make small alterations to the language that is used is this play so as to make it suitable for a younger cast and/or audience.

MUSIC USE NOTE

Licensees are solely responsible for obtaining formal written permission from copyright owners to use copyrighted music in the performance of this play and are strongly cautioned to do so. If no such permission is obtained by the licensee, then the licensee must use only original music that the licensee owns and controls. Licensees are solely responsible and liable for all music clearances and shall indemnify the copyright owners of the play(s) and their licensing agent, ORiGiN™ Theatrical, against any costs, expenses, losses and liabilities arising from the use of music by licensees. Please contact the appropriate music licensing authority in your territory for the rights to any incidental music. In Australia and New Zealand, contact APRA AMCOS apraamcos.com.au.

If you are in any doubt about any of the above then contact ORiGiN™ Theatrical.

For complete listing of plays and musicals available to perform and all licence enquiries, contact ORiGiN™ Theatrical.

---

www.origintheatrical.com.au
+ 61 2 8514 5201

AND HERE ARE THE RULES
IN PLAIN ENGLISH FOR YOU...

BY THE SAME AUTHOR

Dark Voyager

Harp on the Willow

Lip Service

The Shoe-Horn Sonata

Peace Train: The Cat Stevens Story

Sky

AUTHOR - JOHN MISTO

John Misto has been writing plays since 1992. His play, *The Shoe-Horn Sonata* has been reprinted nineteen times and sold more than sixty thousand copies. *The Shoe-Horn Sonata* also won the NSW Premier's Literary Award for Best Play and the Australia Remembers National Playwriting Prize.

Misto's other works include *Dark Voyager* about the turbulent relationship between Joan Crawford and Marilyn Monroe. Misto also wrote the hugely successful play, *Harp on the Willow* which won the Rodney Seaborn Award for Best Play. John Misto is co-writer of *Peace Train: The Cat Stevens Story* which has enjoyed several successful national tours of Australia.

John Misto's most recent play, *Lip Service* had a sell-out season at London's Park Theatre in 2017 (under the title *Madame Rubinstein*) and a successful season at Sydney's Ensemble Theatre and at the Lawler Theatre in Melbourne. *Lip Service* has had successful seasons in Prague (in Czech translation) and in Ekaterinburg (in Russian translation) also under the title *Madame Rubinstein*. It is the first play by an Australian playwright to be performed in Russia.

John Misto is also an established scriptwriter and his telemovies and scripts have won many awards including the Queensland Premier's Literary Award, three Australian Film Institute Awards, three Australian Writers' Guild Awards and a Gold Plaque at the Chicago Television Awards.

John Misto has degrees in Arts and Law from the University of New South Wales.

"History is that which has happened - but
is not generally known to have happened."

- Hal Porter

REVIEWS

Premiere Production: *Gossamer* was performed professionally at the Ensemble Theatre, Sydney in 1995, and Fortune Theatre, Dunedin in 1998.

WRITER'S NOTE

This play is based on actual events. Some of these events are so astonishing that the audience can be forgiven for thinking I made them up. However history and biography can verify the following:

In 1920, Sir Arthur Conan Doyle actually published a book called 'The Coming of the Fairies' in which he insisted that fairies existed and that two little girls had photographed them. The book destroyed his reputation.

The Cottingley photographs were examined by dozens of experts – men who had exposed other frauds routinely. No one could explain them, not even the Bank of England's Forgery Investigators. For over seventy years they remained inexplicable.

Towards the end of her life, one of the girls, Frances, implied that the photos were not genuine. Yet she never gave a satisfactory explanation as to how she and her cousin Elsie fabricated them.

Conan Doyle's visit to Australia, in 1920, to lecture on spiritualism, was an incredible success. Thousands greeted him wherever he went. Most Australian newspapers refused to write about Sir Arthur's visit because his views had been denounced by the Church.

All details concerning Sir Arthur's lectures, work, and theories are true. The well-known Australian Sensitive, Charles Bailey, really existed and impressed Sir Arthur greatly.

For several years Sir Arthur and Harry Houdini enjoyed a fascinating but turbulent friendship. The details concerning

Houdini are true. He also visited Australia where, according to his biographers, he was the first man to officially fly an aeroplane on this continent. During his escape from the bottom of the Yarra River he dislodged the body of a suicide – and the shock nearly caused him to drown.

Houdini, like Sir Arthur, was obsessed with the Cottingely photos. Houdini became vehemently anti-spiritualistic. He spent his life "unmasking" clairvoyants. Ironically he died on Halloween – Feast of the Spirits – after being punched in the stomach by his biggest fan. His wife claimed he sent her a sign from beyond the grave.

For reasons no one has ever been able to explain, Houdini bought America's first electric chair – after it had been used to kill five people. He had the largest occult library in the world and took hundreds of X-Rays of his body.

In 1926, the year Houdini died, the real Frances made a visit to America.

The attempt by the young Princess Elizabeth to leap from the royal box and join the fairies is true. The details concerning the Palace intruder in 1982 are true, as are the descriptions of the Queen stamping her foot on the wooden bridge.

CHARACTERS

SIR ARTHUR CONAN DOYLE (60) - A world famous author and expert on the spirit world. He is smart, surprisingly modest, down-to-earth and sincere.

HARRY HOUDINI (45) - A world famous escape artists and stuntman. Houdini is the ultimate showman. He sprays ether on his audiences so they are too dulled to see through his tricks. Houdini is cynical, tough and a bitter enemy of spiritualism. He has a Hungarian accent.

FRANCES GRIFFITHS (15) - A young, naive girl, honest and trusting. Also doubles as BETH.

ELSIE WRIGHT (14) - Cousin of Frances, young, innocent, fun-loving.

FRANCES WADE (80) - The adult Frances Griffiths, smart, alert and no longer trusting. Frances Wade looks like a sweet old lady, but appearances are often deceptive.

EDWARD LOVATT (20s) - An MI5 agent, youngish, eager, and not as clever as he needs to be.

MRS. BETH HOUDINI - Harry's cynical, long-suffering wife. Beth longs to hang up her performing tights and retire but Harry will not let her. Beth has no illusions about fairies.

CHARLES BAILEY (20s) - Charles really existed. He is a well-know Australian "sensitive", capable of contacting the spirit-world and receiving gifts from them via his rectum. One of the gifts includes a small wax bust of John the Baptist. Also doubles as **THE MASTER OF CEREMONIES** and **JIM WHITEHEAD**.

JIM WHITEHEAD (20) - American, superficially charming but also quite lethal.

THE PLAY

ACT ONE

A small bedroom in the Camelot Nursing Home, London, in the 1990's. No luxury here – a small bed, a table, an old fashioned (commode) chair and an upright wardrobe.

Someone is knocking on the door. Not too loudly. No answer. More knocking. Then the door opens slowly and a man (Lovatt) peers around, then enters the bedroom.

Lovatt might be a burglar. He certainly acts like one. He looks around the room, opens the table's drawer, then drops to his knees to search under the bed.

Not having found what he's after, Lovatt opens the wardrobe. Inside he finds Mrs Frances Wade, 85, who has been hiding in there. It is hard to say who is more shocked.

FRANCES: (IN TERROR) Aahh!!

LOVATT: (UNPLEASANTLY SURPRISED) Aaahhh!! (HOLDING HIS CHEST & GASPING) Oh my God – oh my God –

FRANCES: (STAYING IN THE CUPBOARD) What are you doing?

LOVATT: (SITTING) Trying not to have a heart attack.

FRANCES: You were fingering my personals!

LOVATT: (GASPING) You know what I'm looking for.

FRANCES: (PASSING HIM MONEY) Here. It's all I have.

LOVATT: It's not your money I want.

Frances looks appalled. She shuts herself back in the cupboard.

FRANCES: (CALLING OUT) Help! Rape!

LOVATT: (ALARMED) Sshh – sshh – don't *say* that. Please!

FRANCES: (CALLS IN TERROR) Rape!

LOVATT: (DESPERATELY TALKING TO THE CUPBOARD DOOR) M'am – m'am – I don't know who you are – but my whole *life's* in your hands. (If) You yell like that, I'll lose this job, And without a job I can't pay rent. I'll end up living in a park until I'm kicked to death by skin-heads...

FRANCES: What are you doing in my room?

LOVATT: The matron sent me.

FRANCES: You're not on staff.

LOVATT: I started this morning.

FRANCES: Where's your uniform?

LOVATT: Soaking in Napi-san. I was feeding Major Bruckman up in Geriatric Care. I think he was re-living the Battle of Britain.

FRANCES: He was a gunner in the air-force.

LOVATT: Well the Luftwaffe arrived along with the soup. So he threw the bowl at me. He might be senile but his aim's still good.

FRANCES: (OPENING THE CUPBOARD SLIGHTLY) Well if Matron sent you, what does she want?

LOVATT: (TACTFULLY) She thinks some cups and saucers might have wandered in here from the kitchen.

FRANCES: She said that?

LOVATT: Not quite. *Her* exact words were – "There's enough china in that cupboard to open a Wedgewood factory."

FRANCES: (MUTTERS) Cow.

LOVATT: Will you let me take a look in there – please?

Frances opens the door reluctantly and steps out.

FRANCES: Go on.

LOVATT: (SLIGHTLY NERVOUS) You won't shut it – will you? I can't stand being locked in anywhere.

As Lovatt searches, Frances sits on the commode chair.

LOVATT: Why were you hiding in here?

FRANCES: I thought you were bringing my tablets. I refuse to take a Mogadon until it's dark outside. Matron likes us all in bed by four so she can sit in her office and watch "Home & Away". She doesn't even come out for cardiac arrests.

LOVATT: (STEPPING OUT EMPTY HANDED) I guess she was wrong – about the china.

Lovatt looks at the commode chair.

LOVATT: Would you mind?

FRANCES: Nothing's private any more.

But Frances gets up. Lovatt lifts the lid – looks inside – and looks at Frances.

FRANCES: (WITH DIGNITY) They were there when I moved in.

And Lovatt produces a whole stack of china – along with a bottle of whiskey.

FRANCES: I'd offer you some – but you don't drink, do you?

LOVATT: (AMAZED) How did you –?

FRANCES: Not a single burst vein on the whole of your nose.

LOVATT: That's very observant.

FRANCES: (MODESTLY) Oh it's elementary Mr –

LOVATT: Lovatt. But you can call me Ed.

FRANCES: I never get familiar with the staff.

LOVATT: (HURT) Sure.

FRANCES: Don't be offended. Please. I know things can't be easy for you now – what with your divorce and all.

LOVATT: (STUNNED) How on earth –

FRANCES: (POINTING TO LOVATT'S RINGLESS LEFT HAND) Wedding ring mark. A woman might take hers off for work – but a man never bothers – unless he's cheating or –

LOVATT: (SADLY) Or his wife's gone to Spain with the dentist – (BITTERLY) – on the money *I* paid for her crowns... You're a regular Sherlock Holmes. How long have you been here – at Camelot?

FRANCES: (HAUNTED) I don't really know any more.

LOVATT: (SYMPATHETICALLY) It must be hard – growing old – having Nature put the boot in.

FRANCES: You remember what's important. The rest just goes – like gossamer.

LOVATT: Huh?

FRANCES: Those little webs you see on the grass – they say they're left by fairies.

LOVATT: The only things the fairies leave are condoms in the park.

Suddenly there is a loud and ominous click at the door.

LOVATT: (ALMOST SPOOKED) What was that?

FRANCES: Just matron – locking up.

LOVATT: 'Struth! She's locked me in.

And Lovatt hurries to the door.

LOVATT: (CALLS) Hello out there – Matron? (TO FRANCES) Why can't she hear me?

FRANCES: Because she's raced down the hall to watch "Home & Away".

LOVATT: (WORRIED BUT HIDING IT) Oh well – no problem – I'll just climb out your (window) – (STOPS IN DISMAY)

FRANCES
Aren't the bars beautiful? This century's contribution to architecture.

LOVATT: (EDGY) I don't like being... confined in small places.

FRANCES: She'll be back sooner or later. I usually get a toilet break between "Sons &. Daughters" and "Heartbreak High"... What did matron tell you about me?

LOVATT: Not much... She mentioned you'd been friends with some writer.

FRANCES: (OFFENDED) Sir Arthur Conan Doyle was more than "some writer". (HOLDING UP WHISKEY TUMBLER) *This* was a present from him – from his trip to Australia in 1920.

LOVATT: (NOT LISTENING &. GETTING PANICKY) They shouldn't lock old people up.

FRANCES: Oh they don't do this to *everyone*. Just me.

And Lovatt looks at Frances uneasily.

FRANCES: Didn't matron "fill you in" – about Sir Arthur and myself?

Lovatt shakes his head – with dread.

FRANCES: Odd... She never tires of telling people how I was the one who killed him.

LOVATT: (ALARMED) That isn't very funny.

FRANCES: Perhaps she's getting forgetful, poor dear. Let's hope she remembers to let us out.

LOVATT: (POUNDING ON THE DOOR) Matron! Matron! Anyone!

Frances, meanwhile, calmly puts the stolen china back in the commode –

FRANCES: Sshh, Mr Lovatt. Not so loud. You don't want to lose your job. (SITTING ON THE COMMODE SEAT WITH A TUMBLER OF WHISKEY) Isn't this nice!

LOVATT: (YELLING DESPERATELY– AT THE DOOR) Help! Rape!!

FRANCES: (HAPPILY) I haven't had a visitor for ages.

And Frances downs her whiskey.

Darkness

ACT ONE   SCENE 2

A fanfare of trumpets – from the opening bars of The Lion in
    Winter.

It is 1920. Sir Arthur Conan Doyle strides onto the stage of the
    Sydney Town Hall.

He is an earnest, imposing man, an ex-boxer. Sir Arthur is not a
    polished orator but he knows how to speak from the heart.
    And this is the reason for his world- wide success. He
    wears a black arm-band. Sounds of applause greet his
    entry.

CONAN DOYLE: My dear, dear friends! I am stunned by the
warmth of my welcome here – to the shores of sunny
Australia.

MALE HECKLER'S VOICE: Go home you pommie twit!

CONAN DOYLE: I'm not here as the writer of Sherlock
Holmes but as an ordinary man on a spiritual quest. Yet I
was told that I'd find Sydney to be the most spiritually
barren place on earth.

MALE HECKLER'S VOICE: You haven't been to
Melbourne, mate!

CONAN DOYLE: I was warned that your journalists would boycott my talks – that your clergy would denounce me and order all Christians to stay away from my lectures. Yet thousands of you have risked damnation and filled this Sydney Town Hall tonight. Why? Because all of you know just what it is like to open your doors to the telegram boy – to hear him say "I'm sorry" as he hands you the orange envelope... with those dreaded words inside – "His Majesty regrets to inform you... "

On the screen – faces of soldiers, young soldiers, innocent and smiling in family portraits. The last one shows a handsome corporal.

CONAN DOYLE: This – (BRAVELY) this is Kingsley, my son, the joy of my life, killed, at Pozieres. (VERY CALMLY) I died there with him...

Another face appears – a sergeant – slightly older –

CONAN DOYLE: (UPSET BUT IN CONTROL) My brother, Innes, gunned down at the Somme. A part of *me* perished there too. For our gallant dead, the war is over. But not for us. For us there is only grief. But what if it were possible to glimpse our loved ones on the Other Side – as we strained to glimpse those fine young men when they marched away to fight? What if we could raise them up as Jesus once raised Lazarus?

WOMAN HECKLER'S VOICE: Heretic! Blasphemer!

Other voices on the soundtrack support or shush her.

CONAN DOYLE: This is 1920, madam. Would you burn me at the stake?

Another photo appears on the screen. It shows a "refined" English woman. The photo is unremarkable – except that it also contains the fuzzy form of a man in long white cricket flannels. He is standing beside the seated woman.

CONAN DOYLE: All over the Empire we are being bombarded with signs and signals from the world beyond. (HOLDING UP A PAGE) A letter from Mrs Ernestine Mitchell, mother of the well-known English batsman. (READS) "When my son was fighting overseas, he begged me to have my photograph taken as he longed for one to look at. On the very day I did this, Phillip was killed at Verdun. A few weeks later I collected my photo. I was quite surprised to see him in it. Yes, Sir Arthur. My late son Phillip, is standing beside me, dressed in his flannels and blazer. I cannot explain how he came to be there – but oh, as his mother – what a comfort to know (WITH SINCERITY) that even though he might be dead, Phillip still plays cricket for England!"

A mixed response from the unseen audience. Some cheers. Some heckles.

CONAN DOYLE: The spirits are there. They are trying to reach us!

And now we see Young Frances and Elsie playing on Cottingley Glen in England.

FRANCES & ELSIE: (CHANTING AS THEY SKIP) *"My mother said/ I never should/ play with gypsies/ in the wood".*

CONAN DOYLE: From all round the world we are getting reports – of lights in the sky – of mysterious objects. There can only be one explanation. Our loved ones on the Other Side are desperate to make contact. Who knows where or when they'll next appear?

FRANCES & ELSIE: *"My father said/ if I did/ he'd hit my head/ with a saucepan lid".*

The lights dim – eerie music on the soundtrack –

CONAN DOYLE: Let us all join hands and call to our loved ones. Let us ask them for a sign of recognition.

A strange sound. Suddenly Frances looks up and says –

FRANCES: (ALMOST STARTLED) What was *that*?

ELSIE: What?

FRANCES: (CONCERNED) There – in the bush.

ELSIE: Probably just a badger.

FRANCES: Badgers don't fly.

ELSIE: (ALARMED) Frannie – leave it alone! It might be a zeppelin!

But Frances does not hear her. She is staring straight ahead in fascination. Elsie joins her. The two little girls stand side by side, almost mesmerised by what they see.

CONAN DOYLE: (TO SYDNEY AUDIENCE) Do not be alarmed if you suffer a heart attack. The Town Hall ushers carry bottles of cologne. They will sprinkle it on your face to revive you!

12

We hear Lovatt calling out –

LOVATT: Fire! Fire!! – That matron must have a heart of stone. (TO OLDER FRANCES) I'm sorry – you were saying?

OLDER FRANCES: (CONTINUING HER STORY) We ran all the way home – in a state of almost – shock. We just *had* to tell Pa what we'd seen in the bushes. But all he cared about was our feet. He looked down at them and said (GRIMLY) "Your best Sunday shoes. They're soaked right through."

And now we see Young Frances and Elsie, still on stage, breathless.

ELSIE: (TO THE UNSEEN PA) We must have... run through the stream to escape them.

LOVATT: Them?

OLDER FRANCES: The fairies.

ELSIE: They were chasing us.

LOVATT: (TO OLDER FRANCES) The *what*?

ELSIE: It's *true*, Uncle. Honest. There are fairies on Cottingley Glen.

OLDER FRANCES: I could tell (that) Pa was angry. He brought out his camera – he'd won it at the fair – and *demanded* a photo of our fairies – or else! He told us to be back in half an hour.

13

LOVATT: Mrs Wade – I – don't wish to be rude – but if you go round telling tales like that – no wonder they're locking you up.

OLDER FRANCES: (OFFERING WHISKEY) Here. It might calm you down.

LOVATT: (AT THE DOOR) Matron – Matron!

And now Young Frances stands on stage. Elsie is with her.

YOUNG FRANCES: (LOUD WHISPER) Little Things! Little Things! We've brought you bread and sugar.

ELSIE: Come and play with us. Please.

OLDER FRANCES: Do you think I'd *lie* to people?

LOVATT: Not *lie*, exactly. You're like my Gran. She confuses life with television – and she's a big fan of The X Files.

Suddenly we hear an eerie, chilling sound – like wings flapping in the night. Lovatt jumps up. The Older Frances hears it – and so do Young Frances and Elsie.

LOVATT: What was that?

OLDER FRANCES: Nothing, Mr Lovatt. Nothing *you'd* believe in.

Lovatt picks up the whiskey glass – and gulps its contents down.

Now the Young Frances faces the audience, She holds the Midg camera with shaking hands. An eerie wind. The light begins to change. And then, with a supreme effort of will, the Young Frances starts to take her photographs.

A lighting effect accompanies each click of the camera. Then gradual darkness...

ACT ONE   SCENE 4

A blur of light, bright but out of focus, appears on the screen. It remains throughout the scene.

The Young Frances and Elsie stand close together on stage. Frances is peering at something – as if looking through the crack in a door.

ELSIE: Can you see him? Where's he up to?

YOUNG FRANCES: (PEERING) He's just washed the film.

OLDER FRANCES: Pa developed the photos himself. He'd been learning how to do it from a book he'd bought for sixpence.

YOUNG FRANCES: Now he's hanging up the negatives. Once the air dries them out, he'll see everything.

ELSIE: (NERVOUSLY) Quick – let's run.

YOUNG FRANCES: That'll only make him angrier. He'll give us *twice* the hiding.

ELSIE: (SADLY) I wish we'd kept our shoes dry... What's he doing now?

YOUNG FRANCES: He's... (HESITATES BRIEFLY) taking off his belt. (BRAVELY) He's only good for five or six blows – and then his back gives way.

And suddenly we hear Pa's Voice booming out angrily –

PA'S VOICE: (ANGRILY) Frances!! Elsie!!!

It is clear that Pa has just seen what the photos contain. A terrified Elsie buries her head in Frances's protective arms.

And now the blurring light slowly comes into focus. It is the first fairy photograph – literally drying and forming before our eyes.

On the soundtrack we hear the Introduction to Also Sprach Zarathustra by Richard Strauss. If possible, Conan Doyle, Lovatt, the Older Frances and the two young girls should slowly stand up on stage and watch in amazement as the photograph takes shape.

As Strauss's thunderous drums reverberate in our ears, this is what we see –

A photo of Young Frances, her right hand beneath her chin, staring innocently at the camera (and therefore at us). In front of Frances there are four fairies. One fairy is playing a flute. The others could very well be dancing.

The greatest mystery of the twentieth century has just begun...

Lovatt looks at the photo of Frances & the Fairies in an album. At the same time we see it on the screen.

LOVATT: (SLIGHTLY IMPATIENT) They've been cut out from a book.

FRANCES: My father's words exactly. Then he tossed them away and thrashed us both.

LOVATT: Matron!

FRANCES: But when no one was looking Mother saved them from the rubbish. She wiped away the potato scraps – and mailed them to Sir Arthur.

LOVATT: Conan Doyle?

FRANCES: (NODS, THEN WITH REGRET) If only we'd known, we would have stopped her – just taken our beatings and never told a soul.

LOVATT: (POINTING TO PHOTO) Sir Arthur can't have been fooled by *that*. If they were real, you'd be looking *at* them. You're just staring at the camera.

FRANCES: Some creatures are scared of eye-contact. You don't know much about wild things, do you?

LOVATT: I'm beginning to learn why they die in captivity... Do you tell your family they lock you up?

FRANCES: (FONDLY) My husband was a lot like you. Didn't believe in our photos either. "Come on," he'd say, "how'd

17

you *do* them?" (SADLY) (It) Was a stroke that took him. It's a fairy term – *stroke* – they stroke their hands across your head until they've paralysed the brain. (GLARING AT LOVATT) It's how they punish non-believers.

LOVATT: I wish you wouldn't say that. I already have a headache.

FRANCES: *You* don't believe in fairies, do you?

LOVATT: (UNNERVED) Why won't the matron come?

FRANCES: (DRINKING) For the very same reason she's locked the door. They terrify her, Mr Lovatt.

LOVATT: *They*?

FRANCES: Why do you think she sent *you* to fetch the china?

LOVATT: (FIRMLY BUT NERVOUSLY) Look – there's no one in here but you and me.

Frances passes him an envelope with a letter inside it.

LOVATT: (READING THE ENVELOPE) "Forgery Detection Squad – Royal Bank of England" – (LOOKS PUZZLED)

FRANCES: Sir Arthur asked them to analyse our photos.

As Lovatt reads the Bank's analysis aloud, we see the other photos that Frances and Elsie took – four photographs of themselves cavorting with the fairies of Cottingley Glen. They appear, one by one, on the screen.

LOVATT: (READS) "Dear Sir Arthur, The Bank has magnified the Cottingley photos to 500 times their original size. If they'd been cut out from a book with scissors or a razor, their edges would be jagged. But the outlines of them all are incredibly clean and smooth. Whilst the Bank does not *believe* in fairies, you are urged to treat these creatures with caution – and to avoid financial dealings with them."

Lovatt looks up, astonished.

FRANCES: (HAUNTED) It was meant to be a simple game – something to do on a dull afternoon. But there's one tiny problem about playing with fairies. They don't know when to stop. An afternoon – or seventy years – it's all the same to them.

LOVATT: (UNNERVED, PANICKY, PULLING ON THE DOOR) If your fairies are real – make them open *this* up!

FRANCES: Be careful, Mr Lovatt. Sometimes they give you what you want – and you can never give it back!

Then slowly the door creeps open.

Is it necessary to mention that Lovatt looks shocked?

ACT ONE   **SCENE 6**

London, 1921. Sir Arthur Conan Doyle moves onto the stage pushing a small trolley in front of him. The trolley rattles with its load. It is covered with a cloth.

19

CONAN DOYLE: (TO HIS AUDIENCE) How happy I am to return to London – and to all my friends in the Spiritualist Movement. I can say – in all modesty – that my tour was quite a triumph. Australians are a simple but affectionate race who cannot get enough of the English. And now I'd like to share with you some of the treasures I acquired there.

And with a flourish Conan Doyle removes the cloth covering to reveal several very modest items – which he proceeds to hold up and describe.

CONAN DOYLE: (WITH ADMIRATION AND TENDERNESS – AS IF THESE THINGS WERE ALL PURE GOLD) An ash-tray shaped like a palm-leaf... A hand-carved wooden kangaroo – notice its exquisite detail!... A green whiskey tumbler – and a small wax bust of St. John the Baptist... (LOOKING AT THEM LOVINGLY) These things were all hand-crafted by the Dead – and sent from the Other Side... Oh I'm sure the cynics are smirking – but I was there when they arrived – at a séance in the Sydney suburb of Toor-moora! (NOT WITH A FLOURISH BUT WITH REVERENCE) And tonight I have brought along the man who delivered them – the Great Australian Sensitive, Mr Charles Bailey...

A spot-light reveals a man, standing up, in a trance-like state, and wearing nothing but a canvas bag which comes up to his chin. (This should be as eerie as possible.)

CONAN DOYLE: Sceptics have accused him of hiding things on his person. But beneath this canvas, Mr Bailey is naked!

Gasps from the London audience. Bailey swoons and rolls his eyes. Some frothing at the mouth would also be nice. He

20

*does not look comic. Instead he is very spooky and
convincing.*

CONAN DOYLE: (IMPRESSED) Some quiet – please – Mr
Bailey is "receiving".

*Conan Doyle leans closer to listen to Bailey who mutters barely
audible and sometimes garbled words in his trance-like
state.*

CONAN DOYLE: (TO AUDIENCE) He says... he is...
receiving a gift for Mrs Linda – no – *Lydia* Stephens –
from her dead brother Roger... And Roger says to tell you
– "Happy Birthday Lydia!!!"

*As Conan Doyle says these words, Bailey's gasps, his eyes roll
back and his hand shoots high into the air. He is clutching
a small but very tacky vase (or whatever).*

*We hear Lydia Stephens shriek in horror. Then a thudding sound
as she collapses.*

CONAN DOYLE: (CALMLY) I think Mrs Stephens might
have need of some cologne.

*Conan Doyle takes the tacky vase from Bailey and looks at it
with awe and admiration.*

CONAN DOYLE: (EARNESTLY) How could *anyone* who's
witnessed this deny that spirits exist?

Suddenly Houdini calls out –

HOUDINI: Easily! (AS HE STRIDES OR OTHERWISE
APPEARS ON STAGE) Your man's hiding this junk on

him *somewhere.* (REACHING ACROSS TO REMOVE THE CANVAS BAG) Let's have a look –

Gasps from the crowd.

Conan Doyle stands in front of Houdini – blocking him.

CONAN DOYLE: Sir – I inspect Mr Bailey before each session.

HOUDINI: Personally?

CONAN DOYLE: Yes.

HOUDINI: Thoroughly?

CONAN DOYLE: Of course!

HOUDINI: *Everywhere?*

CONAN DOYLE: (PEEVED) I am a doctor by profession.

HOUDINI: (LOOKING AT THE ARTEFACTS, THEN AT BAILEY) Well I'll bet you fifty bucks there's a part of *his* anatomy that's fuller than the last lifeboat off the *Titanic*.

CONAN DOYLE: (OUTRAGED) No man alive could possibly fit (INDICATES ARTEFACTS) *all of that* up his –

*Horrified cries from refined women in the London audience.
   Meanwhile a very worried Bailey rolls his eyes and moans.*

CONAN DOYLE: (TO HOUDINI) I trust Mr Bailey implicitly. You can examine him if you wish.

HOUDINI: (PULLING UP A CHAIR) Your Sensitive's looking tired. He should take a load off his feet.

CONAN DOYLE: (CALMLY BUT FIRMLY) Charles – can you hear me? Tell the Spirits you need to sit down.

But a very worried, swooning Bailey replies –

BAILEY: The Spirits say I must keep standing.

CONAN DOYLE: Tell them it's important!

HOUDINI: To hell with your Spirits!!

And suddenly Houdini grabs Bailey and pushes him down into the chair.

Bailey shrieks in (understandable) agony, clutches his stomach and sinks to the ground in his canvas bag.

Conan Doyle looks with dismay at the vase he is holding – then puts it down and wipes his hand.

CONAN DOYLE: (GENUINELY DISILLUSIONED) Oh my... oh my...

HOUDINI: Australians! They're still a race of crooks and convicts. (EXTENDING HIS HAND IN FRIENDSHIP) It's a pleasure to meet you, Sir Arthur! My friends call me Harry. Harry Houdini.

On the screen we see a black and white photograph showing skeletal trees in bleak, wild grasslands. (The photo is called 'Fairy Site in Sussex' and is found on page 25 of 'Fairies').

At the same time we see the Older Frances is looking at her photos – and drinking.

FRANCES: Oh they laugh when they say it *now*. But once the very word made people lock their doors and tremble. To hear your neighbour whisper *fairy!* was like... being in a London pub when someone cries out – (WITH FEAR) "I.R.A.!" You could never be sure what might happen next. Nothing. Or your worst nightmare.

A bleak wind howls.

ACT ONE   SCENE 8

A few hours later... Conan Doyle and Houdini have just entered Conan Doyle's London house. They are in the middle of a heated discussion.

CONAN DOYLE: Twenty three stitches! Mr Bailey almost died.

HOUDINI: I just wish I'd pushed him harder!

CONAN DOYLE: (HURT) Why do you wage this – war – against us?

HOUDINI: (COLDLY) If the Spiritualists are honest, they have nothing to fear from me.

CONAN DOYLE: (ANNOYED) Of course we're honest! (RELUCTANTLY) *Most* of us...

HOUDINI: Not one of you has ever proved the Other Side exists. All you and your people do is feed on the grief of others.

CONAN DOYLE: Now wait a minute – !

HOUDINI: The day my father was buried, my mother went straight to a spiritualist – so she could tell my Papa what a wonderful funeral he'd missed. The man charged her five dollars. All the money we'd saved for rent. We had to sleep out in the street for days – thanks to a spiritualist. That's when I vowed to tell the world just what you lot are up to.

CONAN DOYLE: You didn't sabotage my speech to help your fellow man. You knew damn well it would make the morning papers – in the very same week your show opens in London.

HOUDINI: Are you implying something, Sir Arthur?

CONAN DOYLE: No. I'm saying it to your face! I do not like being exploited for publicity.

HOUDINI: (ANNOYED) That's not why I came to your talk. I'd heard rumours about some photographs – of supernatural creatures. I thought you might be showing them.

CONAN DOYLE: They're not for public viewing.

HOUDINI: (EAGERLY) But they do exist?

CONAN DOYLE: (NODS) And you'll never see them. No one makes me look a fool twice over!

HOUDINI: *I* wasn't the one who made you look like a fool. Mr Bailey got there first. Save your anger for *him*!

CONAN DOYLE: (ANGRILY) If I'm angry, sir, you'll know it! I was Heavyweight Champion of St Paul's College.

HOUDINI: (DELIBERATELY GOADING HIM) English boxers...

CONAN DOYLE: Perhaps you'd like to see one in action!

And Houdini lifts his shirt to reveal his abdomen. He bares it defiantly at Conan Doyle.

HOUDINI: (ANNOYED) As if I'd need you to get my name in the papers. When I'm already world famous for *this*! (AS HE POUNDS HIS OWN STOMACH) Here – take your best shot – go on! But if you can't make me blink, you must show me those photos.

When Conan Doyle begins to hesitate –

CONAN DOYLE: Now wait on a minute –

HOUDINI: So you don't have faith in English boxing after all?

CONAN DOYLE: (GETTING ANGRY) By golly – you are pushing me.

HOUDINI: (THUMPING HIS STOMACH) Then let's see what sort of man you are: Strike me on the count of three.

CONAN DOYLE: It's my duty as a gentleman to warn you of my record –

HOUDINI: (BREATHES IN DEEPLY) One!

CONAN DOYLE: (RAISING HIS FIST) Fifteen knockouts – undefeated.

HOUDINI: (BREATHING IN AGAIN) Two!!

CONAN DOYLE: (THREATENINGLY) Nine bare-knuckle street fights!

HOUDINI: (WITH VENOM) Three!!!

A pause. Houdini and Conan Doyle look at each other. Then Conan Doyle fakes a punch, leading with his left fist but suddenly striking hard with his right. His punch lands right on Houdini's stomach.

Houdini's eyes widen with pain. He gasps. He wheezes. But Houdini does not blink.

CONAN DOYLE: (WATCHING TO SEE IF HOUDINI BLINKS) Amazing. Absolutely amazing. (SOMEWHAT REMORSEFUL NOW HE'S NOT ANGRY) Oh, my dear fellow – I'm most dreadfully sorry.

HOUDINI: No...That was... good...

CONAN DOYLE: Your rectus abdominus is quite incredible...

HOUDINI: (GASPING) I... withdraw my remark about... English boxing...

And Houdini extends his hand. Conan Doyle shakes it.

CONAN DOYLE: (NOT AWARE THAT HE WAS BAITED ALL ALONG) And perhaps *I* was a little hot-tempered...! apologise... (THEY SHAKE HANDS)

HOUDINI: Sir Arthur – you noticed that I didn't blink. Which means I get to look at them. The photos.

CONAN DOYLE: (RELUCTANTLY) Yes... Yes I suppose you do...

Conan Doyle turns to get them. Once he is out of sight, Houdini doubles over in agony, muttering in Yiddish and clutching his stomach.

And Conan Doyle holds his fist and rubs the knuckles "Damn... damn... damn."

Then Conan Doyle returns with the photos – but hesitates.

HOUDINI: I give you my word – I will not denounce them publicly.

CONAN DOYLE: Then why are you so keen to see them?

HOUDINI: Whenever a new trick appears, I have to learn its secret – or I wouldn't be able to call myself the greatest magician in the world.

Conan Doyle passes the Cottingley photos to Houdini – along with a magnifying glass.

CONAN DOYLE: I've already had them tested... And the experts are astounded. Perhaps – at last – we have some proof that spirits *do* exist.

HOUDINI: (GRIMLY) Who took these?

CONAN DOYLE: *They* did. (POINTS TO PHOTOS) The two young girls. I'm to visit them next week.

HOUDINI: Incredible... These really are astonishing.

CONAN DOYLE: "And a little child shall lead them."

HOUDINI: (VERY GRAVELY) But this is not the work of children, Sir Arthur...Why I've never seen anything like it. You're dealing with a gang of experts here. Criminal masterminds. (OMINOUSLY) They could well be the best in the world...

And as Houdini utters these words, we see – and hear – Young Frances and Young Elsie skipping and chanting in a most uncriminal fashion –

YOUNG FRANCES & YOUNG ELSIE:
Teddy Bear, Teddy Bear, had a bowl of cream.
Teddy didn't like it so he gave it to the Queen.
Queen didn't like it so she gave it to the King.
King said, "Shut your eyes and count sixteen!"
One – two – three – four...

And the skipping fades...

ACT ONE   SCENE 9

On the screen we see a painting called "The Fairy Raid" by Sir Joseph Noel Paton from pages 10 –11 of "Fairies".

Lovatt faces the audience. He is a very different Lovatt to the one we saw in Scene 1. He is firm, tough, in control. And he is addressing a small, unseen group.

LOVATT: Some background notes about these creatures: Nobody knows where they first came from. It is said that the Vikings brought them to England – to help them conquer us. Before each battle, the fairies fed them mushrooms – which sent the Viking warriors wild – so they felt neither fear nor pain. They called these magic mushrooms *berserk*... Like us, the fairies have a queen. Her crown is said to be made from tears – crystal tears – dropped from the eyes of ravaged girls and writhing brides... We call homosexuals fairies because once it was believed that the Wee Folk kidnapped boys – as slaves – and replaced them with creatures who were of their own kind... So now that you know what we're up against, I'll conclude this briefing with a story – not from any book but from this Organisation's Classified files.

And now we see some photos of the youthful Princess Elizabeth.

LOVATT: (READS FROM A FILE MARKED TOP SECRET) September, 1937. The Princess Elizabeth attends a performance of "A Mid-Summer Night's Dream" at Covent Garden. Shortly after the lights go down, she moves to the edge of the Royal Box, thirty feet above the stage. She calmly climbs up onto the railing – throws her arms wide – (EXTENDING HIS ARMS AS IF TO FLY) – and prepares to jump. Just as she is about to step out, her bodyguard sees her –

And now, on the soundtrack, we hear a Man's Voice calling – "No! Look out!"

30

LOVATT: (CONT) – and grabs her by the ankles. When asked why she had tried to jump, the Princess replies that the fairies made her do it. There were fairies in the play – flying round on the stage. They called to her in beautiful voices – urging her to join them. It is the closest she has ever come to death... If you liked that tale, here's another one for you –

And now a photo of Michael Fagan appears on the screen.

LOVATT: (GLANCES AT FILE AGAIN) July 7th, 1982. The night this man decides to break into... the most tightly guarded fortress in England. He is spotted scaling an outer wall – and the alarm is raised at once. As the sirens wail he calmly strolls past four lots of sentries. Nobody stops him. Within minutes he has reached the main building. Windows, which are double-locked, glide upwards to his touch. Soon he has found the private suite of the head of this entire complex. He opens a bedroom door with ease and the watch-dogs lick his hands. Then he sits on the bed and says in the darkness (CALMLY BUT OMINOUSLY) "M'am – M'am – time to wake up. You have a visitor."

And now, on the screen, we see a photo of the Queen.

LOVATT: (CONT) Later he is charged with *Stealing Wine Whilst Trespassing*. He – Andrew Fagan – an unemployed plumber – is asked how he managed to reach the Queen's bedroom without even a map. "The fairies showed me," is what he said. "They were very obliging." (CALMLY) But this quote was never published in The Times. Her Majesty asked that it not be printed...

Darkness...

On the soundtrack we hear some of Rossini's La Gazza Ladra –
the section that occurs about four minutes into the piece –
a section of flute and strings – music that is impish and
mocking and mischievous. Fairy music.

On the screen all sorts of drawings appear showing the powerful
and sometimes frightening inhabitants of the fairy kingdom
– not cute, winged creatures – but grim, troublesome and
alarming spirits.

As the lights come up, Conan Doyle is interrogating Frances and
Elsie. Elsie clutches a biscuit but is too nervous to eat it. A
pot of jam is beside her.

CONAN DOYLE: I get letters every week from people who say
they've seen ghosts or... fairies... And if I believe them –
and it turns out I'm wrong – I get into trouble. Serious
trouble.

ELSIE: Will they lock you up?

CONAN DOYLE: Much worse than that. Worse than being
burned alive. Worse than having your heart ripped out and
left for the dogs to eat. They'll laugh at me.
(OMINOUSLY) Do you know what gossamer is?

The girls shake their heads in terror.

CONAN DOYLE: It's the web a fairy spins. It looks like silk –
it's so smooth and fine – but once you're caught in its tiny
threads, it cuts your flesh like coils of barbed wire – and
the more you struggle, the more it tears – till in the end
you're bleeding and helpless. A lie is like a gossamer

web... Once you begin, there is no way out... (PUTTING HIS ARMS AROUND THEM) Now I don't care if there aren't any fairies. All I want to know is – how did you take those photos? (TEMPTINGLY) Come on, Elsie. You can tell Uncle Arthur.

FRANCES: I'm Frances.

CONAN DOYLE: (SLIGHTLY TOUGHER) Do you want to see me carted off – put into stocks – and laughed at?

The girls shake their heads in terror.

CONAN DOYLE: (VERY TOUGHLY) You used paper cutouts, didn't you? And strung them up with cotton threads?

The girls nod, terrified.

CONAN DOYLE: Liars! (INDICATES THE PHOTOS) See those wings – that fairy's wings – why they're transparent!

FRANCES: (ALARMED) Transparent?

CONAN DOYLE: It means you can see right through them. Look – there's a tree right behind them – and a waterfall – just like over there. You couldn't see that if the fairies were faked. Paper wings are not transparent!

Elsie, by now, is hiding behind Frances.

CONAN DOYLE: (GETTING ANNOYED) Other men have seen your photos. Men from the Bank of England. I asked them what they thought and they said "Genuine. Authentic. Amazingly real!" Those fairies could be many things but *never never* cut-outs! (MUTTERS IN DISGUST) Do you

33

know what happens to deceitful little girls? They are locked in the Tower of London – (GRABBING THE BISCUIT FROM ELSIE) with nothing but bread and water. At supper time you can hear the wails of crying, lying children!

Conan Doyle rises in anger and disgust. Frances and Elsie cling to each other, petrified. As he is about to exit, Frances calls after him desperately –

FRANCES: We used... peach jam to... bring them out.

ELSIE: (SCARED) They love the taste of sweet things.

Conan Doyle turns around.

FRANCES: I put it on my fingers and let them have a nibble – while Elsie took the photos.

And Elsie nods desperately.

ELSIE: We didn't mean to cause any trouble. We're sorry. Really we are.

FRANCES: Don't lock us up! Please, Uncle Arthur!

CONAN DOYLE: (TENDERLY) Lock you up! You girls are more precious than – than the Crown Jewels of England! (AMAZED, OVERWHELMED, AND ALMOST TO HIMSELF) There really *is* a spirit world – and you two can see it. (WORKING IT OUT DEDUCTIVELY) Your... *auras* allow their forms to be... transferred onto a film – which is why you can photograph them when they're not even visible to my naked eye.

The girls nod helplessly,

CONAN DOYLE: (DELIGHTED) Oh Sherlock Holmes would have loved this! Come here! Come here! (HUGGING THEM) Don't be afraid. You are far too important to be troubled by fear... (HOPEFULLY LOOKING TOWARDS THE GLEN) Are there – any – out there – *now*?

ELSIE: No sir!

But Frances can't help noticing that Conan Doyle seems disappointed.

FRANCES: Wait a minute...I think I saw one – over there!

CONAN DOYLE: (EAGERLY) Where?

FRANCES: Ssshhh! You'll scare it...

This is a very serious moment. Not comic.

CONAN DOYLE: (LOOKING AHEAD ANXIOUSLY) What does he look like?

FRANCES: Like the one in the photo...

ELSIE: His little wings are – *trans-berent.*

FRANCES: Now he's creeping towards us.

CONAN DOYLE: (AWED) I heard the grass rustle. (EXCITEDLY POINTING) Is he over there?

FRANCES: Ssshhh...Ssshhh... (THRUSTS THE POT OF JAM AT HIM AND WHISPERS) Dip your fingers in it. Quickly!

ELSIE: He's coming closer!

FRANCES: Now hold out your hand.

CONAN DOYLE: (THRILLED) He's not – he wouldn't – !!

ELSIE: Don't shout – or you'll scare him.

This moment must be as chilling and as creepy as possible.

FRANCES: Look – here he comes –

CONAN DOYLE: Does he have a name?

ELSIE: Um – yes... His name is –

FRANCES: Little Thing.

CONAN DOYLE: (SLOWLY, AS IF ADDRESSING A TAMED SAVAGE) Greetings, Little Thing. I am called Arth-ur.

FRANCES: He looks like he's smiling.

ELSIE: I think he likes you.

CONAN DOYLE: That's not his – tongue I feel?

FRANCES: Yes, Sir Arthur. He licking the jam.

CONAN DOYLE: (CLOSE TO TEARS) Oh my... oh my... (WITH RAPTURE) He's tickling!!

Conan Doyle stares at his sticky hands. It is hard to believe that an empty space could make a man so sublimely happy. But isn't that what magic is all about?

ACT ONE   **SCENE 11**

Frances watches with some irritation as Lovatt cleans her room. Perhaps Lovatt is on a little step-ladder. Frances is wearing a very bright cardigan – but seems oblivious to the fact that the cardigan is inside out.

FRANCES: (WAVING AWAY DUST) I wish you wouldn't *do* that!

LOVATT: "Spick and span!" Those were Matron's orders... Just wait till you see the dining room. Linen napkins. Flowers on the table. There's even a show after lunch.

FRANCES: (SOURLY) You mean line-dancing done in walking- frames.

LOVATT: Now don't be like that. Won't it be nice to see your children?

FRANCES: They're not coming.

LOVATT: (TACTFULLY) Well – Mother's Day's pretty commercial. They probably don't *believe* in it.

FRANCES: It's *me* they don't believe in...

LOVATT: (RE-ASSURINGLY) Oh I wouldn't say –

FRANCES: It's true. Can't say I blame them. When they were kids they'd come home from school – black eyes – torn clothes – in tears. I was their mother – I should have stopped it –

LOVATT: Stopped what? I don't (understand) –

FRANCES: Every play-ground bully for miles around used to lie in wait and pick on them. Parents too. And teachers. All because of me – because their mother was *the fairy woman*! (CALMLY, WITHOUT SELF-PITY AS SHE PUTS ON SOME MAKE-UP RATHER BADLY) I always knew the day would come when they... realised their lives would be easier without me... I couldn't protect them, Mr Lovatt. So I don't deserve a Mother's Day.

LOVATT: (GENTLY) Was it... like that for Elsie too?

FRANCES: (NODS) Till she died...

LOVATT: (TACTFULLY) It's time to go down to lunch – so you might want to fix your – (cardigan).

FRANCES: Nothing wrong with my cardigan.

LOVATT: No. It's lovely. But it would look even *nicer* if it wasn't inside out.

FRANCES: Don't patronise me, thank you. (FIRMLY) It's meant to be like this. The Little Things are angry. If you wear a garment inside out, it drives them away – for a while.

LOVATT: A sight like that would send Stevie Wonder scurrying... Why are the fairies angry any way? Or don't they like Mother's Day either?

FRANCES: (HEADING FOR THE DOOR) Something's been upsetting them. (VAGUELY THREATENING) And when they're in a temper – well – there's no telling *who* they'll attack. Will you lock up when you're through?

LOVATT: Hang on! You can't go down to lunch like that. Matron will have my hide... (FIRMLY) You'll have to wear that cardigan like Laura Ashley intended – I mean it Mrs Wade – until the Mother's Day crowd have all gone home.

FRANCES: But what about the fairies?

LOVATT: I guess we'll take our chances.

FRANCES: (PUTS IT ON THE RIGHT WAY) Don't say I didn't warn you... They've been waiting for this all day,

A pause. Lovatt looks around – and for just a few seconds he seems a little nervous. These moments should feel as creepy as possible. But then Lovatt relaxes.

LOVATT: See! (MORE CONFIDENTLY) See!... (RUBBING IT IN) Did the ground open up? Did the ceiling fall in? (SCORNFULLY) Cardigans inside out! That's nothing but an old wives' tale. (WITH RELIEF – AS HE MOVES HIS LADDER OFF-STAGE AND CLIMBS ON IT) If everyone behaved like *you*, we'd be back in the jungle fighting monkeys for bananas.

Then suddenly we hear – and if possible see – Lovatt's ladder
collapse beneath him. Lovatt crashes to the floor. He lies
there unconscious. And as the lights fade we hear the
sounds of frenzied, chattering monkeys...

ACT ONE   SCENE 12

On the soundtrack we hear "The March of the Trolls" by Grieg
– fast-paced, ominous, wickedly vibrant music.

At the same time theatrical posters appear on screen – posters
advertising famous magicians of the 1920s: "Thurston's
Astonishing Floating Woman" "The Bombay Marvel",
"Ivan – the Bullet-Proof Man!".

On the stage is a large, upright trunk. But we are looking at this
trunk from behind because the trunk is facing an imaginary
1920s theatre audience.

MASTER OF CEREMONIES: (STANDING WITH HIS
BACK TO US & ADDRESSING THE 1920s
AUDIENCE) Please welcome to the Empire Theatre that
King of Handcuffs and Monarch of Leg Irons – the Great
Houdini!

Applause. The spotlight shines on Houdini, in chains, as he
enters an upright trunk and the Master of Ceremonies
locks it.

MASTER OF CEREMONIES: (DRAWING A CURTAIN
AFOUND IT) The Great Houdini *swears* to escape in
under six minutes – or all admission monies will be
refunded!! Gentlemen – please – feel free to smoke.

A drum roll. From inside the trunk we can hear desperate, grunting sounds and the rattling of chains. (Houdini really used to do what follows).

Unseen by the 1920s audience, but clearly seen by us, Houdini crawls out through a fake panel at the back of the trunk. He moves to the side of the stage, near the trunk, but where the 1920s audience cannot see him.

A chair and a glass of beer have been left there. There is a heavy chain beside the chair. Houdini begins to enjoy his beer as the Master of Ceremonies says –

MASTER OF CEREMONIES: Houdini begs for your patience and your prayers!

Then Conan Doyle appears behind Houdini.

CONAN DOYLE: Well done!

HOUDINI: (SURPRISED TO SEE HIM) Sir Arthur!

CONAN DOYLE: I slipped the door-man half a crown. You don't mind if I join you?

HOUDINI: Please – (INDICATES SEAT) I'm honoured. Oh – be careful –

And Houdini indicates an old-fashioned insecticide sprayer on the chair.

CONAN DOYLE: (HOLDING IT UP) Fly spray?

HOUDINI: No. It's ether... If the audience gets too wild or impatient, my assistant squirts it in the air. Calms them down in no time.

CONAN DOYLE: Incredible... (LOOKING AROUND, SLIGHTLY EDGY) I say – we can't be *seen* up here?

HOUDINI: No – it's totally private.

CONAN DOYLE: Good. I don't want them to know we've spoken.

HOUDINI: Them?

CONAN DOYLE: I'm being followed.

HOUDINI: By who?

CONAN DOYLE: (SHRUGS) At first I thought I'd been working too hard. Shadows glimpsed by moonlight – footsteps in the fog – that's the kind of thing I write about. (POINTING TO 1920s AUDIENCE) But I'd hardly call those two out there a product of my imagination.

HOUDINI: Where?

CONAN DOYLE: Right at the back,

HOUDINI: (PEERS OUT) You must go to the police!

CONAN DOYLE: They haven't broken any law. They haven't even spoken to me. Besides, I don't think they're criminals. They're not dressed well enough.

HOUDINI: Then I'd walk down the aisle and demand to know just what the hell they're doing!

CONAN DOYLE: That's what they want – I'm sure of it... I've seen them drive away sometimes – in an automobile. An Oldster. So I wrote its number down – and asked a friend of mine in Scotland Yard to trace it. I didn't tell him why.

HOUDINI: And?

CONAN DOYLE: (CALMLY) The Oldster belongs to the government.

HOUDINI: (SURPRISED) What!?

CONAN DOYLE: That's all he'd tell me.

HOUDINI: But why would the government want to tail you?

CONAN DOYLE: Because of... the photographs.

HOUDINI: Come on, Sir Arthur. You can't be serious. You think Westminster gives a damn about a couple of cardboard fairies?

CONAN DOYLE: They would if they were real. Think about it, Harry. Suppose those creatures are from the Spirit World.

MASTER OF CEREMNIES: (V/O) Houdini? Can you hear me? Please let us know if you're still alive!

HOUDINI: (TO CONAN DOYLE) There are no spirits!

Then Houdini picks up the chain beside him, rattles it and moans as if struggling.

43

CONAN DOYLE: What if those girls have really made contact? In a couple of months we might... we might actually talk with the dead.

HOUDINI: That's like – going to the moon! It will never, never happen!

MASTER OF CEREMONIES: Harry – keep it down! (FOR AUDIENCE) Three minutes remaining, Ladies & Gentlemen.

CONAN DOYLE: Imagine the secrets the dead could divulge – the plots – betrayals – assassinations! What government would be safe?

HOUDINI: If you're such a big threat, they'd have killed you straight off.

CONAN DOYLE: Not if I've hidden the photos. That's what they're after. The evidence. They're hoping I'll lead them to straight to it.

HOUDINI: Then what can you do?

CONAN DOYLE: There's only one way to end this, To get them off my tale. Bring it all out in the open. Publish the photos.

HOUDINI: Sir Arthur... You can't... People think of you as Sherlock Holmes – they trust you.

CONAN DOYLE: So?

HOUDINI: If you tell them you believe in fairies –

MASTER OF CEREMONIES: (V/O) Two minutes remaining. Harry, shift your butt!

CONAN DOYLE: The experts will support me. Kodak's. Eastman's. The Bank of England.

HOUDINI: (INDICATING 1920s AUDIENCE) But what about them? What will they say? (WITH URGENCY) Take a good hard look at your public. Have you ever seen so many dead eyes – slack jaws – or wide open mouths...? They are the ones who will judge your photos.

CONAN DOYLE; The British are a fair and rational nation. They'll give me a chance to explain my position –

HOUDINI: They'll turn on you like dogs on a deer! Go home, Sir Arthur. Burn your fairies. If you publish those photos – I promise you – in a hundred years time (POINTS TO 1920s CROWD) they'll still be laughing!

MASTER OF CEREMONIES: (V/O) Thirty seconds – Harry – move it!

Houdini reaches out and takes Conan Doyle's hand.

HOUDINI: (WITH GREAT SINCERITY) It would be a great pity if you were destroyed. This world needs honest men like us.

Then Harry Houdini begins to make himself look dishevelled – so it will look as if he has been struggling to escape from the trunk. Then Houdini slips back into the trunk – through the fake back panel – as the Master of Ceremonies appears on the 1920s stage and prepares to draw back the curtains around the trunk.

MASTER OF CEREMONIES: (V/O) Nine – eight – seven – Houdini can you hear me? Six – five – four – three – two – one –

Then Houdini emerges from the trunk – appearing to be triumphant but exhausted from the effort. With his back to us, Houdini faces the wildly cheering 1920s audience and bows. On the soundtrack we hear, once again, The March of the Trolls – the music of mischief and mayhem...

ACT ONE   **SCENE 13**

We hear groaning sounds. Lovatt stirs. The Older Frances hovers over him. The room should be dark and eerie looking – perhaps, in the distance, distorted sounds from the line-dancing. Frances is wearing her cardigan inside out again.

LOVATT: (GROANS) Ow...Oww...

OLDER FRANCES: It's all right; Mr Lovatt.

Lovatt touches his head – then sits up alarmed.

LOVATT: Oh my God – that's blood?

OLDER FRANCES: No. You bumped your head. So I put some butter on it.

Lovatt looks at Frances, puzzled.

OLDER FRANCES: Your ladder collapsed. Don't you remember?

46

Lovatt shakes his head, then looks straight ahead and says –

LOVATT: (PUZZLED) Who's that laughing?

OLDER FRANCES: (SHRUGS) Must be downstairs...

LOVATT: (TRYING TO STAND) I really ought to –

OLDER FRANCES: You should stay where you are for a while.

LOVATT: (GRIMLY) It wasn't them – understand? That ladder is old – it broke.

OLDER FRANCES: I didn't say a word.

Lovatt, meanwhile, grabs the whiskey bottle and takes a long swig.

LOVATT: And we'll talk about something else besides fairies.

OLDER FRANCES: Whatever you like.

LOVATT: That's the trouble – you dwell on one thing – you pick at it over and over. I bet Sir Arthur was like that too. Got. obsessed – couldn't leave it alone.

OLDER FRANCES: I suppose so. Yes. Looking back.

LOVATT: I'll bet – as soon as he left your house – it was the only thing he could think about.

OLDER FRANCES: (NODS) A few weeks later he sent Pa a telegram – wanted us to come up to London. Of course we were all excited.

47

And now we see Elsie, in her best Sunday dress, weeping her heart out. Young Frances does her best to console her. They are in a hall. A dais is nearby.

YOUNG FRANCES: Sshh – sshh –

ELSIE: Who'll curl my hair if I'm in gaol? There'll be no one to look after my dolls!

YOUNG FRANCES: I'm sure you can bring some with you. And maybe if we ask them nicely, they'll lock us up together.

Then Young Frances, too, begins to cry. And at this point Houdini appears, almost out of nowhere.

HOUDINI: I hope you two aren't going to wail all through Sir Arthur's big announcement. Here –

And Houdini produces a silk handkerchief – almost out of nowhere. Elsie is so impressed she stops crying. She reaches out to take the handkerchief – but Young Frances restrains her.

YOUNG FRANCES: (POLITELY TO HOUDINI) We're not allowed to take gifts from strangers.

HOUDINI: If you called me "Uncle Harry", I wouldn't be a stranger.

Now Houdini magically divides the silk handkerchief into two – giving one to each of the girls.

HOUDINI: Now why are two such pretty girls crying?

ELSIE: (SADLY) We're going to prison, Uncle Harry.

HOUDINI: (QUITE SERIOUSLY) Wormwood Scrubs or Broadmoor?

YOUNG FRANCES: The Tower.

HOUDINI: (IMPRESSED WHISTLE) Who did you kill? Lloyd George?

YOUNG FRANCES: Worse. We took photos.

ELSIE: Of fairies.

YOUNG FRANCES: They'll tell us that we're lying.

ELSIE: And liars get sent to the Tower.

HOUDINI: (VERY KIND & RE-ASSURING)
Now...now...cheer up... (BRIGHTLY) Why the Tower's not too bad. Oh the rats might bite for the first few weeks but the cells are so dark you won't even see them.

More sobbing from the girls. So Houdini "magically" produces more handkerchiefs.

HOUDINI: Still – I'm sure if you told me the truth right now, I could have a few words with a couple of judges and you'd get off with a warning.

ELSIE: You think so?

HOUDINI: Absolutely!

The girls nod at this idea and wipe their eyes.

49

HOUDINI: (VERY TRUSTING TONE) So why don't you tell your Uncle Harry how the fairies got into your photos?

Frances and Elsie look at each other uneasily. Houdini tries to remain calm.

ELSIE: We put them there.

HOUDINI: No! (BARELY ABLE TO RESTRAIN HIMSELF) And how did you do that?

YOUNG FRANCES: Peach jam.

ELSIE: They love peach jam.

YOUNG FRANCES: They'll go anywhere for it.

ELSIE: Uncle Harry – you're hurting!

HOUDINI: (SLIGHTLY ANNOYED & HUGGING THEM EXTRA TIGHTLY) I said that I wanted the truth... (GRIMLY) This – technique of yours – who developed it?

YOUNG FRANCES: (NOT UNDERSTANDING) Pa did. In his dark room.

HOUDINI: (TO HIMSELF) Yes... of course...That's why he's setting Sir Arthur up. He stumbles on a way to revolutionize photography. Then he hoodwinks a famous figure – so he can publicize his invention. (TO FRANCES) He's a clever man, your father.

FRANCES: (POLITELY) Yes. He is.

ELSIE: (POINTING) That's him – up there.

HOUDINI: (WITH URGENCY) It might not be too late. (TO ELSIE & FRANCES) Tell him – I'll pay him – he can name his own price. But he has to warn Sir Arthur – now – that fairies don't exist.

FRANCES: (ALARMED) I can't... remember all that.

HOUDINI: (URGENTLY) Say that Harry Houdini's here and must talk to him at once!

ELSIE: (TO FRANCES, AS THEY LEAVE) Harry – who?

And Frances shrugs. Suddenly the spotlight falls on Conan Doyle who is standing at the dais.

CONAN DOYLE: Ladies and Gentlemen. Members of the Press. I am here to announce a major discovery – an event of such magnitude that words alone simply cannot do it justice. What makes this more incredible is that two young girls are responsible for it...

On the soundtrack we hear an excited buzz from Conan Doyle's 1920's audience. Houdini, meanwhile, waits anxiously for the girls to return.

CONAN DOYLE: To the sceptical among you let me say – the photographs you are about to see have been thoroughly tested and analyzed.

OLDER FRANCES: We ran to Pa as fast as we could. We said someone called Harry had asked to see him.

LOVATT: And?

51

OLDER FRANCES: Pa shoo-ed us away. He threatened to spank us later for talking to strangers.

CONAN DOYLE: The results are clear and unambiguous. These images are real. Photograph One – Frances & the Fairies (AND WE SEE IT ON THE SCREEN) – taken in July on a sunny day with a Midg Quarter camera.

But as Conan Doyle speaks, gradual laughter fills the auditorium.

CONAN DOYLE: (INDICATING FAIRY WITH FLUTE) Notice the wingless nature spirit is playing some kind of pipes. The Cottingley life-forms clearly possess a highly developed intelligence. I discuss this at length in my latest book – "The Coming of the Fairies"...

More heckles as the second photograph appears – Elsie & the Leaping Fairy.

CONAN DOYLE: (BRAVELY) Photograph Two – The Leaping Fairy.

MALE HECKLER'S VOICE: The fairies have leapt on you, Sir Arthur!

CONAN DOYLE: Photograph Three – A Fairy at Her Sun-bath.

Heckles and boos.

CONAN DOYLE: Please! Please! Let me read to you what the experts have said – qualified men who have examined these photos – (READS) "Genuine" "Unfaked" "Completely Inexplicable." Today we have proof – beyond all doubt – that fairies are more than creatures of myth. They are real!

Heckles – jeers – some applause. There is a riot in Conan Doyle's audience.

WOMAN HECKLER'S VOICE: (ANGRILY) Have you never heard of Darwin?!

MALE HECKLER'S VOICE: Go and read some science!

CONAN DOYLE: (GETTING UPSET) What has science ever done for us but strip our lives of hope and joy?

The response to this is outrage.

LOVATT: (TO THE OLDER FRANCES) How did you do it? How did you fake them?

CONAN DOYLE: Who knows what secrets these creatures can reveal about Nature – and Man – and the Other Side?

OLDER FRANCES: We never meant to hurt him!

LOVATT: (GRIMLY) You destroyed him, Mrs Wade. You and Cousin Elsie.

OLDER FRANCES: (WORRIED) You're not yourself. That fall's done this.

LOVATT: What did you do to your little photos? How did you and Elsie fix them?

OLDER FRANCES: I don't like this – you should be quiet – you said we weren't to talk about fairies.

LOVATT: Let's talk about the truth then, shall we? Do you know what that is? Have you ever told the truth?

OLDER FRANCES: (GASPING) Please – Please – I need the matron.

LOVATT: She'll be watching *Home & Away* by now. She doesn't even come out for cardiac arrests. (ALMOST ANGRILY) Where did they come from – your little fairies? Did you put them there or did someone help you do it?

Suddenly a spotlight reveals Young Frances and Elsie, holding hands, terrified.

CONAN DOYLE: These two little children have unwittingly made the greatest discovery in human history. They have found – not just a country – but an entire hidden world. (WITH PASSION) In a hundred years time when historians speak... of Christopher Columbus or Vasco Da Gama – in the same breath they will utter the names – Frances Griffiths and Elsie Wright of 31, Main Street, Cottingley!

And the uproar is deafening. "Liar!" "Fraud!" "Idiot!" "Fool!"

The Older Frances clutches her heart and bends forward in agony in her chair. Lovatt realises that she has had a heart attack.

LOVATT: Mrs Wade? (ALARMED) Mrs Wade!... Oh no – Oh God – I didn't mean to – (STOPS, LOOKS UP) who are you? what are you – doing – no – keep away – (RISING IN

ALARM) You hear me? Keep away!! (RINGING THE
BELL & CALLING OUT) Matron! Matron!

Meanwhile, amidst the uproar, Houdini hisses at Young Frances
and Elsie –

HOUDINI: You're both to blame for this! You are wicked,
wicked girls!

CONAN DOYLE: (POINTING DESPERATELY AT THE
PHOTOS) Ladies & Gentlemen – let me finish! If you'd
just let me finish I know you'd understand. The Cottingley
fairies could change our lives. They could teach us things
we have only dreamed of.

LOVATT: (IN TERROR) Matron! Matron! Get them off me!!!

CONAN DOYLE: Quiet! Quiet! I beg you – please! Today is
the greatest day mankind has ever known! For on this day
we can truly say that the fairies are here. And they are real!

LOVATT: (WAVING HIS ARMS AROUND IN TERROR)
Get them off me – someone get them off me!!!

CONAN DOYLE: They are real! Can't you see? They are
real!!!

Lovatt desperately tries to keep the fairies away as Young
Frances and Elsie weep in terror. Conan Doyle puts his
arms around them protectively as the (unseen) audience
explodes in an uproar of abuse and derision. Perhaps some
things are thrown at them.

And Houdini walks among the audience with his fly sprayer –
angrily spraying them with ether fumes.

On the screen we see the front cover of the most controversial book of the 1920's – "The Coming of the Fairies" by Sir Arthur Conan Doyle.

On the soundtrack we hear the frenzied music of Camille Saint-Saens Danse Macabre as we see several more drawings of fairies – those creatures of mischief and terrible deception...

INTERVAL

ACT TWO

AMERICAN ANNOUNCER'S VOICE: Reach for your
smelling salts, Lovers of Magic! The Great Houdini is
proud to present his sensational new act – An Escape from
the Very Same Guillotine that was Used to Behead Marie
Antoinette!

We hear "Ooohs" and "Aaahhs" on the soundtrack.

*And now we see Houdini kneeling with his head in a very simple
suggestion of a lunette (the lower part of a guillotine). We
do not need to see the blade or anything elaborate. But
there is a small basket beneath his head – (to catch it!) and
it is lined with newspapers. We can see the edges of the
newspapers... Houdini is able to raise his head, lower it,
and move it from side to side. But he is forced to stay
kneeling because he is handcuffed and cannot free his
hands to release his head from the guillotine.*

*Mrs Houdini is locking him in. She is dressed as a magician's
assistant – in garish netted tights, sequins, feathers – the
whole kaboodle. She does lots of smiling, gestures and
flourishes.*

AMERICAN ANNOUNCER'S VOICE: Is everything ready,
Mrs Houdini?

And Mrs Houdini nods and gestures.

HOUDINI: (TO HIS WIFE) Did you get the evening paper?

MRS HOUDINI: (STILL SMILING – BETWEEN
CLENCHED TEETH) Do I ever forget? It's in the basket.

AMERICAN ANNOUNCER'S VOICE: Then in three minutes time this blade will descend – (MRS HOUDINI INDICATES THE BLADE) – and no power on earth can stop it!!

MRS HOUDINI: (AS SHE DEPARTS) And tonight don't laugh at the funny pages. It destoys the atmosphere.

A drum-roll. Mrs Houdini exits. A spotlight falls on Houdini.

Meanwhile we see Mrs Houdini sitting off-stage. (We can see her but the 1920's audience cannot.) She is still in her outfit – but, like her husband, clearly bored by these brushes with death. To pass the time she is reading the newspaper and drinking from her hip-flask. She has little interest in what is happening on stage.

Houdini also reads from the newspaper that lines the head-basket beneath him. Mrs Houdini reads from the newspaper in front of her. And now we see Conan Doyle, seated and reading in the comfort of his study – from the same newspaper.

HOUDINI: (WITH INTEREST) Oh... (READS) "Letters to the Editor." Sir – I am writing to deplore Sir Arthur Conan Doyle's announcement that fairies do exist. What on earth is this man up to?

HOUDINI & MRS HOUDINI: (JOINING IN AS SHE READS THE SAME ITEM) "He has jeopardized the safety of a delightful race of creatures. It is bad enough that war and pollution have almost wiped them out."

HOUDINI & MRS HOUDINI & CONAN DOYLE: "But now, thanks to Sir Arthur, British fairies will be hounded

59

by the stupid and the curious. Shame on you, Sir Arthur! (WITH PASSION) Shame!"

AMERICAN ANNOUNCER'S VOICE: Two minutes and thirty seconds remaining!

HOUDINI: How idiotic can people get?!

MRS HOUDINI: (THOUGHTFULLY) That's a very good point!

CONAN DOYLE: (READING) "It is not the habit of the British Press to sensationalize the news but experts have examined these photos and pronounced them to be real."

MRS HOUDINI: (READING) "– even the Great Houdini himself cannot prove otherwise."

HOUDINI: (LOOKING UP – APPALLED) What!! (CONTINUING TO READ) "Is it really possible that two little girls have out-witted the Master of Illusion?" (FURIOUS) Damn those fairies! By the time I'm through they'll be begging for pollution! I'm going down there now and – show them once and for all that –

But it soon becomes apparent that something is terribly wrong with the handcuffs.

AMERICAN ANNOUNCER'S VOICE: Two minutes remaining. And may God have mercy on his soul!

HOUDINI: (TO HIMSELF) That catch – it's supposed to be unbolted. (GETTING VERY WORRIED) If I yell for help, I'll be laughed off-stage. (OPENS HIS MOUTH TO YELL

BUT STOPS.) Mrs Houdini – turn this way. Please! Someone did the bolt up!

AMERICAN ANNOUNCER'S VOICE: Sixty seconds remaining. Would those with heart trouble please leave the theatre now.

MRS HOUDINI: (READING) "In reply to his critics, Sir Arthur has said –"

HOUDINI: Look at me, woman! Or else I'll die!!

Meanwhile Mrs Houdini mouths the words silently as Conan Doyle says –

CONAN DOYLE: (PASSIONATELY, TO THE AUDIENCE) "– I would like to remind you of the words of Charles Dickens – himself a firm believer in fairies. A nation without fantasy never did, never can, never will hold a great place under the sun. Fairies are essential to the survival of the Empire!"

HOUDINI: Mrs Houdini – I'm stuck!

MRS HOUDINI: (READS) Newspapers world-wide have been deluged with letters from people who claim to have seen the (REACHES FOR HER GIN FLASK – AS SHE DOES SO SHE GLANCES AT HOUDINI) Holy Mother of God!!

And Mrs Houdini hurries onto the 1920's stage. But once she is there, she conceals her anxiety behind a great big smile and lots of gestures and flourishes.

MRS HOUDINI: (MAINTAINING HER SMILE) Mr Houdini!

HOUDINI: The bolt – it's jammed.

MRS HOUDINI: Shall I use the fly spray?

HOUDINI: There's no time. Hurry!

AMERICAN ANNOUNCER'S VOICE: Fifteen – fourteen – thirteen –

Mrs Houdini is used to on-stage emergencies. She pretends to mop her husband's brow or fan him and, as she does so, she reaches behind and undoes the bolt.

AMERICAN ANNOUNCER'S VOICE: Four – three – two –

And Houdini jumps up, free. We hear the loud, crashing, metallic thunk of the guillotine blade as it misses him by inches – and seconds. The audience goes wild.

Houdini and Mrs Houdini hold hands and take elaborate bows with lots of blowing kisses and gestures. At the same time, fiercely under their breaths –

MRS HOUDINI: What the hell happened?

HOUDINI: The bolt locked me in! You forgot to undo it. You and your gin. You could have killed me!

MRS HOUDINI: No. It was loose. I checked it twice. The stage hands watched me. Go ahead – ask them!

HOUDINI: Then who did it up? (SCORNFULLY) The fairies, I suppose!!

For a few brief seconds the Houdini's stop bowing as they look at each other in alarm. Could it be? Is it possible?

Then the Houdinis resume their bows – but not quite as grandly as before...

ACT TWO   SCENE 15

One week later. Lovatt is trying to make Frances have her breakfast.

LOVATT: (BRIGHTLY) You should have seen Matron! Soon as I yelled that you were in trouble, she switched off "Young Doctors" and came tearing in here... Then she took one look and... rushed me off to Casualty.

FRANCES: Did she bother to take my pulse?

LOVATT: She said you're always having turns. Come on now. Try to eat. You don't want matron coming in to force-feed you.

FRANCES: (ANNOYED) You yelled at me. No. More than yelled. You threatened me.

LOVATT: I wasn't in control. The concussion made me do it. They said my brain was bruised. You wouldn't believe my hallucinations. (RUBBING HIS HEAD) I've spent a whole week in bed – with nothing in the house to read but a Barbara Cartland my wife left behind.

FRANCES: How perfect for someone with brain damage.

LOVATT: As soon as I could walk I bought some soccer magazines. And that book Sir Arthur wrote – "The Coming of the Fairies".

FRANCES: I thought you didn't believe in them.

LOVATT: It's a nice bit of folk-lore, that's all. The Druids thought they were a race of Ancient Britons who lived beneath the ground and practised magic. They even called them The Secret Commonwealth. But if they really existed, they'd still be around.

FRANCES: (ANGRILY) Has it ever occurred to you that there's a reason for their disappearance?

LOVATT: Like what? What could make the fairies vanish?

FRANCES: Try genocide, Mr Lovatt. This is the century for it. And they'd be perfect candidates. Trusting and gentle and unprotected. There's no place for creatures like that on this planet. Why the world's so brutal we wouldn't even notice a bit of ethnic cleansing at the bottom of the garden.

LOVATT: But how do you – exterminate a fairy?

FRANCES: Oh we'd find a way I'm sure. It's what we're good at.

LOVATT: (TRYING TO CHEER HER) Sir Arthur was an interesting man. There was a chapter at the end about him.

FRANCES: (IMPATIENT) I'm already quite familiar with the subject.

LOVATT: His father died in an insane asylum. (PROUDLY) Did he tell you that?

FRANCES: (LYING) We had no secrets.

LOVATT: (BRIGHTLY) Sir Arthur campaigned for animal rights – long before it was fashionable. You could almost call him the first English Greenie. He tried to stop feathers being used on British hats. And picketed the fox-hunts.

FRANCES: He had a very kind heart – not an enemy in the world.

LOVATT: (SURPRISED) But he had hundreds, Mrs Wade. The man was hated.

FRANCES: (SHOCKED) By whom?

LOVATT: Well – the Church of England to start with. The clergy blamed Sir Arthur for their dwindling congregations. His talks on the Spirit World were so inspiring, whole families took the first bus home and killed themselves! They'd never done that for the Archbishop of Canterbury!

FRANCES: Yes...I remember. It's... coming back to me now...

LOVATT: But what really sank him was the Titanic.

FRANCES: (SHOCKED) You cannot blame Sir Arthur for that!

LOVATT: He couldn't understand why it had gone down in the first place. So he began to study British ships and...he decided that their water-tight doors just didn't work at all.

FRANCES: (UNEASILY) I think I am a bit hungry now.

LOVATT: (NOT HEARING HER) When he warned the British Admirals they all laughed. And they didn't stop laughing till the U Boats appeared – and one by one our ships went down as their water-tight doors opened wide for the ocean. The German High Command said if we'd listened to Sir Arthur, we'd have won the war by 1916. Our navy never forgave him.

FRANCES: But Sir Arthur was loved – he was mobbed wherever he went.

LOVATT: Oh the masses might have adored him but he made some people nervous. In the year he published your photographs – he'd begun a campaign to get Home Rule for Ireland – a dangerous notion – then and now. Why if he'd lived in America, someone would have gunned him down – some convenient itinerant with five o'clock shadow.

FRANCES: That isn't funny.

LOVATT: (GRIMLY) No. But it's the truth. It's the fate of modern giants – we expect them to be shot. And Sir Arthur was a giant. (CALMLY) Still Cottingley fixed all that. Without a single bullet being fired.

FRANCES: How dare you even imply that I – why you take it back at once!

LOVATT: You can't take History back, I'm afraid. The ridicule killed him. And that's a fact.

FRANCES: (FIERCELY) It's a lie, Mr Lovatt. It's a truly wicked – I had nothing to do with Sir Arthur's death.

LOVATT: (SLIGHTLY SURPRISED) It's in the book – I thought you knew. He lost the will to live. (It's) Like something straight out of the Brothers Grimm. Right at the end – those little fairies – were able to bring down the giant after all...I guess the bottom of the garden is a dangerous place to wander. (CALMLY) More Farex, Mrs Wade?

Frances glares at Lovatt. If looks could kill...

ACT TWO   SCENE 16

A bleak New York morning, just before dawn, 1922. Conan Doyle stands alone in the centre of the stage. He looks around nervously. Then we hear Houdini say –

HOUDINI: It's all right. No one's followed you.

CONAN DOYLE: (SURPRISED & RELIEVED) Harry!

HOUDINI: (AS THEY SHAKE HANDS) Thank you for coming here.

CONAN DOYLE: (HALF-JOKING) I hate being dragged out of bed before dawn. It's why I stopped being a doctor...I'd only ever do this for you. But why in blazes have you asked me to a prison?

HOUDINI: It's the one place in New York where I still feel safe.

CONAN DOYLE: (PEERS AT HIM WITH CONCERN)
You're as white as a sheet! What on earth's the matter.
(NO REPLY) I'm missing out on my tea and toast. The
least you can do is answer me.

HOUDINI: (RELUCTANTLY) Sir Arthur – I ve... never said
this to any one before but... I'm afraid.

CONAN DOYLE: That's nothing to be ashamed of.

HOUDINI: It is for me. I'm supposed to be immune to fear. It's
what I'm famous for. Only once before now have I even
been nervous. In a place called Mel-bourne.

CONAN DOYLE: I've heard that name – it's north of Sydney.

HOUDINI: (NODS) I was performing an escape – in chains. I
jumped into the Yarra River – and sank straight
downwards – just as I like to. But as soon as my feet
touched the bottom – a human head shot up through the
mud. I had landed on top of a drowned man! I wanted to
scream – but I'd have lost my breath. So I...looked him
right in the eyes. I forced myself to beat my terror... But
now...How do I fight what I can't even see?

CONAN DOYLE: What's going on?

HOUDINI: Last month – on stage – I got trapped in my own
guillotine! "All right," I thought. "Accidents happen. From
now on I'll be extra careful." Two days later – I was about
to hang myself – when I found my trick rope had been
replaced with a noose. My assistants raced to get the fly-
spray. But someone had put Mortein in it! Ever since then
everything has gone wrong. I watch my equipment night
and day but – (SHAKES HIS HEAD)

CONAN DOYLE: Do you have any enemies?

HOUDINI: Not a soul in the world. Everyone loves me. I'm worshipped.

CONAN DOYLE: Then who'd want to kill you?

HOUDINI: There's only one possibility. Remember what you said, Sir Arthur? If the dead could talk, no government would be safe. My government knows we're friends. They know about your work. Perhaps they think I'm helping you —

CONAN DOYLE: Sshh! Someone's coming.

HOUDINI: (LOOKING OFF STAGE) It's all right. They won't harm us. I see them every week.

CONAN DOYLE: (PEERING OFF-STAGE) That looks like a priest and...some guards. This isn't a —

Houdini nods. They both look off-stage.

CONAN DOYLE: Poor devil...What's that thing they've just unveiled?

HOUDINI: They call it the Electrified Seat. They'll tie him in and turn on the current...Escape is impossible – so they say.

CONAN DOYLE: How can you bear to watch this?

HOUDINI: I don't have any choice. I'm buying it from the prison – so I have to make sure it works OK.

CONAN DOYLE: You mean – for an escape? You won't get out of that alive!

HOUDINI: It will make me the greatest magician ever!

And now, off-stage, we hear the Voice of the Priest, praying in Latin. His prayers for the dying continue as –

HOUDINI: I was laughed at because of your photos. The papers said that two little girls knew a magic feat I could not perform. Well no one will laugh at me after this... But I cannot have my finest trick sabotaged. Which is why I need your help Sir Arthur.

CONAN DOYLE: Of course. Anything. Name it, Harry.

HOUDINI: Write a letter to The Times. Say you were wrong about Cottingley. Admit there is no Spirit World.

CONAN DOYLE: (APPALLED) You want me to lie?

HOUDINI: I want you to call them off! They're after me because of those fairies. If my government thinks it's all a mistake – they won't feel threatened – they ll leave me alone.

CONAN DOYLE: I just...can't do it. It's...out of the question.

HOUDINI: I'm not the only one those fairies are destroying. Last month you suggested a tunnel get built – between Dover and Calais – and everyone laughed. But once they would have listened to you. Please, Sir Arthur. End this now – before you ruin us both.

CONAN DOYLE: (COLDLY) I will not renounce the Spirit World.

HOUDINI: (UPSET) Spirit World – baloney! Once you die, there's nothing!

PRIEST: (FROM OFF-STAGE) Hey – do you mind? I'm trying to comfort this guy!

HOUDINI: (TO CONAN DOYLE) It's our only hope.

CONAN DOYLE: A gentleman does not lie. I – I'd rather sit in that Electrified Seat and pull the switch myself!

As if on cue the Electrified Seat starts to do its job. It buzzes wildly (off-stage). Blue lights flash and illuminate the stage. The two men, now, are a ghostly shade. They don't even notice.

HOUDINI: (ANGRILY) I refuse to be murdered for some silly cardboard cut-outs!

CONAN DOYLE: And I have no intention of betraying my fairies!

HOUDINI: (FURIOUS) Fine. Fine. Then our friendship is over.

CONAN DOYLE: If that's what you want – consider it done!

HOUDINI: I hope your After-Life exists. You've wasted all of this one on it!

CONAN DOYLE: When I could have been doing such useful things – like kneeling in a guillotine – or filling myself with electric shocks!

71

The sparks keep flying. As Conan-Doyle exits, Houdini calls after him –

HOUDINI: (SCORNFULLY) A tunnel from England to France! The day they do that, even I'll believe in fairies!!

We see a final, angry burst of sparks from the Electrified Seat... Then on screen we see the following headlines appear – Houdini Attacks Sir Arthur! and Spirit Movement Dying!

ACT TWO   SCENE 17

A photo of the Young Frances appears on screen as Lovatt says sternly –

LOVATT: It is not our job to sit in judgment. We have no views. We have no values. We must approach each assignment with a clear and open mind... In 1926 Frances Wade went to New York. She was a nineteen-year old shop-girl who could not afford a trip to London. Why she travelled to America is something of a mystery. But the dates of her visit were carefully noted and locked away at MI6. Something else happened in that same year. Harry Houdini died. As far as we can tell, the two are not connected. (ALMOST AS AN AFTER-THOUGHT) But why did they keep a top-secret file on this harmless girl from Bradford? And why was her every move in New York watched by an agent from MI6? (GENUINELY AMAZED) Did they really think the fairies were a threat to international security?

Gentle, haunting music – something like Danse Arabe from The
    Nutcracker Suite.

As the lights come up, Young Frances is standing at the door of
    Houdini's study in his home in Harlem, New York. It is
    1926.

FRANCES: (UNCERTAINLY) Mr Houdini?

HOUDINI: You used to call me "Uncle Harry". Here –
    (PASSES HER DRINK) I expect you're not used to the
    heat.

FRANCES: Thank you.

HOUDINI: (AS SHE DRINKS) It's called Cocaine & Cola.
    (TRYING TO UNNERVE HER) It's wonderfully
    refreshing – and it cleans the silver too... How is Sir
    Arthur?

FRANCES: (NERVOUSLY) Very well.

HOUDINI: Don't lie to me. He's dying... Perhaps you'd like to
join us for dinner. We're having my favourite – bread and butter
    pudding.

FRANCES: You're very kind but I... can't stay long. I don't like
    walking home in the dark.

HOUDINI: You're perfectly safe in Harlem.

FRANCES: Someone followed me from the station and –

HOUDINI: (WITH SURPRISING INTENSITY) Followed you? A man?

FRANCES: I think so. I mean – I think he followed me. (SUMMONING ALL HER COURAGE) The reason why I came – and I hope this doesn't offend you but – I'd like you to leave Sir Arthur alone.

But Houdini hardly listens. He is too busy peering out the window.

HOUDINI: (AS HE PEERS OUTSIDE) So what do you think of New York? Not a bad place really – apart from the climate and the people.

FRANCES: Those things you've been saying – they're in all the London papers. He gets laughed at wherever he goes. It's bad enough that you're killing him. Can't you let him die in peace?

HOUDINI: I have none. Why should he?

FRANCES: That's not Sir Arthur's fault.

HOUDINI: (TURNING ON HER) He was the one who showed me your photos – who asked for my – expert opinion. That's when it started – that very night. A question began to play in my head – "How did they do it – two little girls? How did they develop a trick that even fooled the Great Houdini?" Five years later the question's still there – pounding now against my brain – until the flesh is black and bruised – how? How?

FRANCES: (SHOCKED) That's why you attack Sir Arthur, isn't it? Because of us – because of what we've –

74

HOUDINI: (CALMLY BUT IN PAIN) Sometimes it makes me think so hard it's – it's like my head is bleeding. (GRABBING HER DESPERATELY) End it for me. Please.

FRANCES: (ALARMED) Uncle Harry –

HOUDINI: You want me to leave Sir Arthur alone? Answer the question. How did you fake the Cottingley photos? I won't tell a soul. I swear it.

FRANCES: (NOT TOO LOUDLY) Let me go.

HOUDINI: You can name your price. (DESPERATELY) My wife has a diamond – the Tsar used to wear it – hold it up to the moon, it brings tears to your eyes... It's yours if you'll tell me.

FRANCES: (MOVING GENTLY TOWARDS THE DOOR) Thank you for the Cocaine & Cola. Now I really must be –

HOUDINI: I have to know before I die. I cannot face eternity with this. (WITH DESPERATE WHISPERED URGENCY) How did those creatures get in your photos? (ASHAMED) I am begging you...

A pause. Frances looks at Houdini. Then –

FRANCES: We...saw them.

HOUDINI: (CALMLY BUT SHOCKED) That isn't fair.

FRANCES: Goodbye.

And Frances leaves.

HOUDINI: (CALLING AFTER HER) I want a proper answer. I deserve a proper answer. There are no fairies. You know that, damn you. Don't do this to me. Please. (ALMOST WEEPING) There are no fairies!!!

On the soundtrack we hear the achingly beautiful Romance from The Gadfly by Shostakovich.

*And now we see Conan Doyle, old, sick and sitting in the moonlight. He dips his fingers into a pot of jam, holds his hand up, looks into his fingertips and smiles with sheer delight. At the same time, headlines on the screen announce – **Controversy Kills Sir Arthur – Thousands Mourn Sherlock Holmes...***

ACT TWO   SCENE 19

Lovatt looks at the audience and begins to speak in an authoritative manner. As he talks, a photo of the Queen gradually appears on the screen.

LOVATT: At one p.m. her Rolls Royce stopped and the Head of the Firm alighted from it. We observed her to walk to one end of the bridge where she started stamping her foot on the wood. She must have hit it at least three times – the sound being loud. Then she turned to her chauffeur and said – "Now they'll let us cross." When questioned, her chauffeur informed us that she always does this – out of politeness – to let the fairies know she's coming.

*October 30th, 1926. The Princess Theatre, Albany. Houdini is
sitting, staring bleakly ahead. Mrs Houdini enters with a
tray of food.*

MRS HOUDINI: (DELIGHTED) It's freezing outside – but
they're queuing for tickets! They'll have to clap just to
keep warm. Here's your dinner.

HOUDINI: Have you talked to the stage hands?

MRS HOUDINI: Your Electrified Seat is all set up. I worry
about this trick sometimes. Filling your brain with voltage
and currents. No wonder you're getting headaches.

HOUDINI: I only had one. Not even a headache. A tiny flash in
front of my eyes.

MRS HOUDINI: You should send the Electric Chair back to the
prison. Let them use it as Nature intended.

An eerie, moaning sounds fill the air. Houdini looks up.

MRS HOUDINI: It's only children. Pretending to be fairies. For
Halloween, remember?

HOUDINI: Send them away!

MRS HOUDINI: I'll get them some candy. (RE-
ASSURINGLY) I wish you'd relax. Not even a spirit could
get through those doors.

*And suddenly a man materializes – almost out of nowhere. He is
clean-cut, All-American lad in his early twenties.*

77

WHITEHEAD: (OVERWHELMED) Mr Houdini – it really is!!

HOUDINI: Who the hell –

WHITEHEAD: Jim Whitehead. I'm a medical student.

HOUDINI: I don't need a doctor and that door says "Do Not Enter!".

WHITEHEAD: Actually it says "Private". Didn't the manager tell you...I was coming?

MRS HOUDINI: No – he did not! And how did you get in here?

WHITEHEAD: Oh Lord – I don't believe it! No wonder you're upset. Last year I caught pneumonia queuing up for one of your shows. The manager said if I survived, he'd arrange for me to meet you. He told me to come here tonight and – I'll get out of your way at once. I'm terribly, terribly sorry.

MRS HOUDINI: (TO HOUDINI) At least give the poor boy an autograph.

Houdini does so.

WHITEHEAD: Gee – thanks. (LOOKING AT TRAY) I'll bet that's bread and butter pudding.

MRS HOUDINI: (SURPRISED) Yes!

WHITEHEAD: (TO HOUDINI) You have it seven days a week. (ADORINGLY) I know everything about you. (CAN'T RESIST SHOWING OFF) Your birthday – 6th of April – favourite colour – black. You were the first man to fly a plane in Australia – you did it in a place called. (STRUGGLES WITH THE NAME) Mel-bourne. (PROUDLY) And you own the largest black magic library in the world.

Houdini and his wife exchange a slightly uneasy look. How does he know this?

WHITEHEAD: (BRIGHTLY) They say you've even conquered Death.

And the Houdini's realise that this man is their Nemesis.

HOUDINI: (CALMLY) Who says?

WHITEHEAD: Oh – you know – the magazines.

HOUDINI: I've never read that. Not in any magazine.

WHITEHEAD: Is it true?

HOUDINI: Why would you care?

MRS HOUDINI: (TRYING TO BE BRIGHT) He's a doctor. He's worried you might put him out of business.

WHITEHEAD: (NICELY BUT FIRMLY) My uncle died and we can't find his will. I'd like to ask him where he left it.

HOUDINI: A magician never gives away his secrets.

MRS HOUDINI: It's been very nice to meet you but –

HOUDINI: (GRIMLY) I've seen you before, haven't I?

WHITEHEAD: I'm always in the audience.

MRS HOUDINI: Thank you so much for coming. Goodbye.

WHITEHEAD: Yes. Goodbye...Oh – I almost forgot. Could I...just have a look at it?

MRS HOUDINI: At what?

WHITEHEAD: (TO HOUDINI) Your stomach... They say a man can punch it and you don't even blink... (SMILES) But that's medically impossible. Like talking to the dead.

HOUDINI: You don't think I can do it?

MRS HOUDINI: Mr Houdini!

HOUDINI: I've been punched a thousand times.

WHITEHEAD: You must be a very brave man.

HOUDINI: (GLARING AT WHITEHEAD AS HE BARES HIS ABDOMEN) Nothing frightens me at all.

WHITEHEAD: (THRILLED) Wow! Those striations are spectacular.

HOUDINI: (CALMLY) You'd like to hit it, wouldn't you? To see what you are up against?

WHITEHEAD: Gosh no. I'm a Quaker. We're not allowed to punch.

MRS HOUDINI: (RELIEVED) Well. What a shame. Good-bye Mr –

WHITEHEAD: Though I guess this isn't really punching. It's more like – testing a reflex. Could I? Would you mind?

MRS HOUDINI: (UPSET) Yes – he minds! He isn't well.

HOUDINI: (FIRMLY TO WHITEHEAD) Do it on the count of three.

MRS HOUDINI: (DESPERATELY TO WHITEHEAD) The voltage gives him headaches. Sometimes he even sees things.

HOUDINI: One!

MRS HOUDINI: Mr Houdini!

But Houdini will not back down.

WHITEHEAD: I just came to...say hello...

HOUDINI: (CALMLY) I know why you came, Mr Whitehead.

And Whitehead begins to crack his knuckles like an expert. And we realise – Quaker or not – he has done this before. A lot.

HOUDINI: Two!

MRS HOUDINI: (SADLY) I guess it must be Halloween. The fairies get up people's noses.

HOUDINI: There are no fairies! – Three!

And suddenly, out of nowhere, a beautiful little fairy appears just above Houdini. Whitehead and Mrs Houdini cannot see it. But we can.

And so can Houdini.

Houdini looks in amazement at this incredible, fluttering spirit.
He follows it for a few seconds, transfixed by its beauty.
Houdini's eyes glaze over and he smiles.

WHITEHEAD: Mr Houdini – I'm your biggest fan.

You cannot blame Houdini for forgetting to tense his stomach
muscles.

Suddenly Whitehead punches Houdini – bam! Right in the
abdomen.

The fairy vanishes on the moment of impact. Houdini drops to his
knees and groans in agony. Mrs Houdini screams.
Whitehead steps back – then turns and hurries off.

All we see now is Houdini – alone in the spotlight – on his knees,
doubled-up in pain – and yet – there is almost a smile on
his face...

As Houdini writhes, we see the newspaper headline proclaim –
"Halloween Horror – Houdini Dies!".

ACT TWO   SCENE 21

Lovatt is taking photos of a very reluctant Frances.

FRANCES: Stop that!

LOVATT: Matron's orders I'm afraid. She wants you on the
new brochure. Try and look as if you like it here.

FRANCES: She wouldn't use me on a brochure - unless she wanted the place closed down. (ANOTHER PHOTO) Stop that!

LOVATT: (AIMING CAMERA) If your dentures aren't in, just say "champagne".

FRANCES: (CALLS) Matron!

LOVATT: (CALMLY BUT WITH MENACE) She's gone off for a sherry with the twenty quid I slipped her.

And Lovatt moves in closer – taking more photos from various angles.

FRANCES: (SUSPICIOUS) What do you want from me, Mr Lovatt.

LOVATT: (ALMOST THREATENINGLY) Help... I want your help. It's why I came to this – hole – in the first place. (GRIMLY AS HE CONTINUES TO TAKE PHOTOS) I work for a Firm – and we're in trouble.

FRANCES: I don't know a thing about business.

LOVATT: We're pretty close to bankruptcy now. It hasn't been our year, you see. It hasn't been our decade.

FRANCES: And I'm not the least interested in –

LOVATT: When I tell you what our trouble is, I'm sure you'll understand –

FRANCES: (IRRITATED BY HIS PERSISTENCE) Matron!

LOVATT: – Bulimia – adulteries – self-mutilation –

FRANCES: (ALARMED NOW) Matron!!

LOVATT: – fires – betrayals – and a little bit of toe-sucking. One *annus horibilis* after another.

Frances stops – as she realises. On the screen we see a photo of the Queen.

FRANCES: (SHOCKED WHISPER) You can't blame me for that. I've never even met her.

LOVATT: A prowler broke into her room. I'm sure you read about it. We don't know how he got there since it's physically impossible. Would you like to know what he said to her –

FRANCES: (ALARMED) I don't want to get mixed-up in –

LOVATT: – what he whispered in her bedroom on that velvet lilac quilt? "M'am", he said, "M'am – you must save Cottingley."

Frances looks at Lovatt stunned.

LOVATT: She's convinced the fairies sent him.

FRANCES: This has nothing to do with me. I haven't been there for years!

LOVATT: They're going to dig up the Glen. Property developers... She intends to intervene and save it. She thinks there might be fairies there – because of you and what you did.

FRANCES: (DEFENSIVELY) Then she's a kind-hearted woman.

LOVATT: Imagine what will happen if the tabloids get wind of this. A monarch who believes in fairies. They'll laugh her off the throne. She's the only family member left with any credibility.

FRANCES: But people would admire it.

LOVATT: Remember when Prince Charles confessed he sometimes talked to plants? It wasn't really plants – just a tomato he'd grown close to. That destroyed his reputation. One little red tomato. People laughed at him for years – even now they haven't stopped. (FIRMLY) We will not stand by and let them ridicule the Queen.

FRANCES: But I can't help her.

LOVATT: Ofcourse you can. She thinks there are fairies on Cottingley Glen. You must tell her the truth – that you faked those photos – that they were a plot to destroy Sir Arthur. Once Her Majesty knows that, she'll leave Cottingley alone.

FRANCES: Did she...send you to see me?

LOVATT: She doesn't even know I'm here. We don't tell her everything. MI6 is accountable to no one.

Frances looks at Lovatt in horror – then dashes for the door. But Lovatt grabs her and drags her back.

LOVATT: Do you want to destroy the House of Windsor?

FRANCES: Let me go! Let me go!

LOVATT: (TOUGHLY) What happened on Cottingley Glen? (TWISTING HER ARM OR SOMETHING EQUALLY NASTY) We'll do this bone by bone if we have to!

Frances gasps – cries –

FRANCES: We – we used peach jam to bait them. They can't resist peach jam. They swoop in low with their huge wings buzzing.

LOVATT: They? Who are they?

FRANCES: Horse-flies. Dozens of them. In no time at all they were trapped in the syrup – and we ripped off their wings – their large, transparent wings. Then we opened up a page of the Princess Mary Gift Book and cut some fairies from it –

LOVATT: (GRIMLY) The experts insisted they could not have been cut out. You're lying, Mrs Wade!

FRANCES: (GASPING WITH PAIN) – and we pasted wings onto the fairies – and when the paste was dry, we strung them up on wire. Thin, thin wire. Gossamer wire.

Lovatt twists her arm again or whatever.

FRANCES: Aaahh – It's true – I swear it – they were hopeless bloody fakes. It was just a game. A childish game. Pathetic little fairies. We laughed and laughed about it. (SHOCKED WHISPER) And then the experts said that they were real...

LOVATT: Why?

FRANCES: We didn't know. We didn't. With each photograph we took, we made it more and more obvious – we left bits of cardboard showing – we stuck hat-pins in the navels. But the more we tried to be caught, the more we got away with it.

LOVATT: Who was helping you? I want their names!

FRANCES: I can't tell you that! (GASPS IN PAIN) Fairies don't have names!

Lovatt looks at her – in disbelief.

LOVATT: You're not trying to say –

FRANCES: You can kill me if you want but it's the truth... It took a while before we guessed – but then we knew. No matter how badly we faked our photos, they came out looking real... Her Majesty is right. They are there – on Cottingley -

Lovatt grabs her angrily.

LOVATT: I'm not Sir Arthur, Mrs Wade. You can't pull that on me. (INDICATES POCKET) I have a tape recorder here – and I'd like you to speak into it.

FRANCES: I don't know what to –

LOVATT: "The Cottingley photos are fakes." That's all you have to say.

FRANCES: The... Cottingley –

LOVATT: (TWISTING ARM OR WHATEVER) Speak up – so Her Majesty can hear!

FRANCES: Please don't make me do this...The Cottingley photos... The Cottingley photos... were cut-outs... Oh, God forgive me...

Frances sobs, coughs, wheezes.

LOVATT: (ALMOST GENTLE NOW) Are you having a turn?

Frances nods and coughs. Lovatt walks over to her pills.

LOVATT: The green ones?

FRANCES: (NODS & GASPS DESPERATELY) Hurry...

Lovatt approaches her with the bottle. Frances goes to take them but Lovatt suddenly holds the bottle up high.

LOVATT: One final question, Mrs Wade... Why did the fairies disappear?

FRANCES: I...don't know. (REACHES OUT DESPERATELY FOR THE TABLETS)

And Lovatt begins to crush her tablets under his shoes.

LOVATT: Pity.

FRANCES: Please – I'll die...

LOVATT: Yes. You will. (HOLDING UP PILL) Lucky last... (GRIMLY) How do you kill a fairy? Come on. You've been so helpful up till now...

FRANCES: They...can't...stand it...

LOVATT: Can't stand what?

FRANCES: Metal... iron... It sends a vibration through the earth. It drives them mad... destroys them.

LOVATT: (GRIMLY TEASING) Mrs Wade? (Are you lying?)

FRANCES: It's true. I swear. It's why we hang horse-shoes over a door. It's why the wars have wiped them out – bullets and bombs and shrapnel. They're terrified of iron.

LOVATT: That's it? Just iron? (AMAZED) We could fix them with a bullet?

Frances nods. As Lovatt passes her the pill, he says –

LOVATT: The government thanks you for your co-operation, Mrs Wade.

FRANCES: Where are you...going?

LOVATT: To Cottingley, of course. With a few divisions of the SAS. Make sure the little blighters don't harass the Queen again.

FRANCES: (SHOCKED) But you don't believe in fairies.

LOVATT: You don't have to believe in something to kill it.

And Lovatt exits.

FRANCES: No! Mr Lovatt – no! Come back! (SOBBING PATHETICALLY) Little Things – Little Things...What have I done?...

ACT TWO   **SCENE 22**

Gradual darkness. Then, at the same time, ominous, powerful drums – and the theme music from Zulu – the heavy, rhythmic music of chaos and inexorable destruction.

At the same time, we see slides of soldiers – guns – and tanks. Interspersed with these are drawings (from "Fairies") of startled fairies of all kinds, shapes and sizes. They are fleeing the attack on their kingdom. Perhaps we hear the sounds of guns – bullets raining down – and the shrill little screams of dying fairies.

Soon it becomes apparent that we are witnessing the terrible destruction of Cottingley Glen...

Then the lights come up on Frances talking to someone. She is quite nervous.

FRANCES: Those cinnamon things were lovely... And thank you so much for letting me see you... I caught a taxi to the Glen. It cost a whole month's pension money. By the time I arrived, it had already started... You could hear them shrieking under the wheels as the tanks turned up the soil – crushing their heads and breaking their backs when the poor little things tried to wriggle away... I raced around from general to general – waving my stick – saying "Stop this at once!" (PAUSE) No, M'am. No. Never mentioned your name. I understand that you can't get involved... But what could I do against soldiers and guns? I told them they were killing fairies. And everyone laughed... Laughter and dust...and then the bullets... (TRYING NOT TO CRY) And when it was done – and all gone quiet – I watched them floating in the air – hundreds drifting this way and that – till the wind came up and scattered them... Not fairies, M'am – just their wings – their large, transparent wings...

A blink of light. Now Lovatt addresses his men.

LOVATT: The Glen we cleared has just been sold to a private corporation. Next month construction is due to commence on the biggest MacDonald's in Yorkshire. To be open for business in 1995. Well I hope the Wee 'Folk like Big Macs. 'Cause not even the fairies can stop British Beef!...

FRANCES: Yes, M'am, of course. I quite agree. You couldn't speak out and save them. (It) might have wrecked your reputation. (LYING) And I'm sure the fairies will forgive you for that. They're not malicious – as you know.

And Frances does her best to curtsey – as we see newspaper headlines of the Queen's litany of disasters – Windsor Castle Burns; Charles & Di to Divorce; Duchess of York – Nude Photos Shock; "I Was Edward's Lover" says Footballer. Is Phillip Unfaithful? Girlfriends Tell All!; The list is really endless...

A slide on screen of Sir Arthur surrounded by little fairies (from Page 38 of "Fairies")

LOVATT: This isn't something I'd tell the Queen – but we still don't know how Frances got away with it – how she and cousin Elsie – on their first go with a camera – could fool the world for eighty years...We'll never even know if there was a plot against Conan Doyle. As soon as he died, his papers were seized by Order of the Court. They have never been released.

Perhaps – someone – unknown to the girls – touched up the photos in order to ruin him. But who it was – or why – remains one of history's question marks.

The best plots leave no traces. (HOLDING UP SOME SLIDES) I developed these an hour ago. Some shots I took of Frances at the Home. You can never have too many photos on a file. Always work on the premise that your superiors can't read.

Lovatt smiles – glances at the slides – and then his look changes from one of amusement to one of almost stunned disbelief as –

We hear Frances calling from her chair. She dips her fingers in peach jam and holds them high in the air.

FRANCES: (GENTLY, SADLY, DESPERATELY) Little Things – where are you? Are there any of you left? Why do we pull the wings off everything? (URGENTLY INTO THE DARKNESS) Come back – Oh please, please – come back!

Lightning sounds... A few seconds pause. Then Lovatt arrives. But now Frances looks almost ethereal – serene yet staring straight ahead. Lovatt is quite agitated.

LOVATT: (TOSSING SOME SLIDES OR PHOTOS NEAR HER) The photographs I took of you – thought perhaps you'd like a look. Everyone's been quite impressed – the head of the Firm even heard about them. She called me in for an interview. She asked me to explain. No – she demanded an explanation. She slammed her hand on the desk so hard she nearly dislodged her tiara. She said ever since we cleared the Glen, nothing's been going right. And then, this morning, her Corgis attacked her.

Lovatt now moves closer to Frances. He is grim, calm and menacing.

LOVATT: She says that I'm to blame. It seems she's had my photographs analyzed – by some computer they use at NATO. You know what that computer said? The photographs I took of you are... "genuine", "authentic" and "completely unfaked". She said I'll never work again – in any job in a Commonwealth country. This is not how a fairy tale's supposed to end, you know. (HOVERING OVER HER) I'm not sure whether to beg you or... beat you. (DESPERATELY) How did you get hold of my camera? What the hell did you do to my film?

And now we see some photographs on the screen. They are the photographs that Lovatt took of a very distressed Frances in Scene 21 – when he forced her to reveal how to kill a fairy.

Now, however, in these recent photos that Lovatt took, we can see some other figures – winged creatures hovering protectively over Frances. As Lovatt begins to weep, we can see them quite clearly. The creatures in Lovatt's photos are just like the fairies in the 1917 Cottingley photographs.

Meanwhile Lovatt grabs hold of Frances to shake her. But she is totally limp in his arms. Lovatt realises, to his horror, that Frances is dead.

Lovatt drops to his knees with Frances in his arms. As he nurses her, Lovatt says with great urgency –

LOVATT: Mrs Wade – wake up – you can't die – you can't! (ALMOST SHAKING HER) I have to know what you did to my photographs – (WITH FEAR) There aren't any fairies. We both know that. (ALMOST SOBBING) Please – Please – tell me there aren't!

The sound of lightning. Then a buzzing noise is heard – a low, buzzing sound like dozens of horseflies heading towards him. Lovatt looks around, then stands up, puzzled.

LOVATT: (SOFTLY BUT WITH A MIXTURE OF TERROR & AMAZEMENT) No... No... You don't exist – you don't...

The sound gets louder and louder and louder. Lovatt dips his fingers into the jam pot, then holds his trembling hand in the air as they head towards him, hundreds of them. Genuine. Authentic. Completely unfaked...

THE END

OTHER TITLES AVAILABLE FROM
ORiGiN™ THEATRICAL

LIP SERVICE
John Misto

In John Misto's hilarious new play, LIP SERVICE, Australian
cosmetics tycoon, Helena Rubinstein, is locked in a power
struggle with rivals Elizabeth Arden and Revlon. When Helena
hires a battle-hardened war-veteran as a personal assistant, her
life is turned upside down. As her professional and family
conflicts reach fever pitch, will the ghosts of her past topple the
world's richest businesswomen? Or will war-veteran, Patrick,
save her from herself?

Inspired by real events, Lip Service is a bright new comedy
where the nails are painted and the gloves are off. Yet when the
lipstick bleeds and the makeup fades, what is there left to hide
behind?

"Gloriously entertaining play.... a comic tour-de-force."
- What'sOnStage (U.K.)

*"Lip Service is a hilarious new play by John Misto.... The
audience laughed at every joke, often to the point where actors
had to pause....The buzz will spread fast."*
- The Music

Casting: 1M, 2F
Full Length Play, Drama, Australian, 1960s, 1950s

www.origintheatrical.com.au

HER HOLINESS
Melvyn Morrow and Justin Fleming

All Mary MacKillop wanted was to live the dream, but to others - the staunch hierarchy of the Roman Catholic Church - she was a nightmare.

What Mary MacKillop didn't count on was the degree of obstruction that would stand in her way - opposition from the very people whose sacred task it was to help her.

And for sure, St Mary MacKillop didn't expect to be humiliated and excommunicated, making it necessary for her to disguise herself and travel to Rome to confront the reigning pontiff, Pope Pius IX, in an attempt to brazen out the storm she endured over the years it took her to found and have recognised a religious order of women who would educate the young of wild and remote places in Australia.

Mary MacKillop was Australia's Martin Luther. The antipodean Thomas More. A woman for all seasons. But *her holiness* (the lower case is deliberate) takes this dramatic narrative in an unexpected direction.

"A confronting, moving and very entertaining piece of theatre"
- Australian Stage

Casting: 11M, 6F
Full Length Play, Historical, Drama, Australian,
19th Century, 21st Century

www.origintheatrical.com.au

FOR ALL ENQUIRIES CONTACT: ORiGiN™ Theatrical
PO BOX Q1235, QVB Post Office, Sydney, NSW, 1230, Australia
Phone: (61 2) 8514 5201 Fax: (61 2) 9299 2920
enquiries@originmusic.com.au www.origintheatrical.com.au
Part of the ORiGiN™ Music Group
An Australian Independent Music Company

www.ingramcontent.com/pod-product-compliance
Lightning Source LLC
Chambersburg PA
CBHW060549100426
42742CB00013B/2498